WISHCRAFT

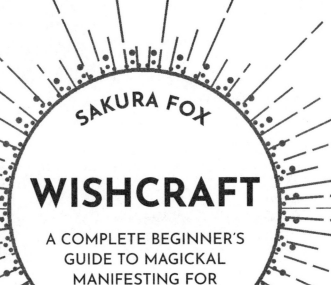

SAKURA FOX

WISHCRAFT

A COMPLETE BEGINNER'S GUIDE TO MAGICKAL MANIFESTING FOR THE MODERN WITCH

HAY HOUSE

Carlsbad, California • New York City
London • Sydney • New Delhi

Published in the United Kingdom by:
Hay House UK Ltd, The Sixth Floor, Watson House,
54 Baker Street, London W1U 7BU
Tel: +44 (0)20 3927 7290; Fax: +44 (0)20 3927 7291; www.hayhouse.co.uk

Published in the United States of America by:
Hay House Inc., PO Box 5100, Carlsbad, CA 92018-5100
Tel: (1) 760 431 7695 or (800) 654 5126
Fax: (1) 760 431 6948 or (800) 650 5115; www.hayhouse.com

Published in Australia by:
Hay House Australia Pty Ltd, 18/36 Ralph St, Alexandria NSW 2015
Tel: (61) 2 9669 4299; Fax: (61) 2 9669 4144; www.hayhouse.com.au

Published in India by:
Hay House Publishers India, Muskaan Complex,
Plot No.3, B-2, Vasant Kunj, New Delhi 110 070
Tel: (91) 11 4176 1620; Fax: (91) 11 4176 1630; www.hayhouse.co.in

A catalogue record for this book is available from the British Library.

Tradepaper ISBN: 978-1-78817-471-8
E-book ISBN: 978-1-78817-472-5
Audiobook ISBN: 978-1-78817-555-5

Interior illustrations: 48, 50, 57, 59, 66, 67, 68, 113, 114: www.jadehodesign.com;
all other illustrations: Shutterstock

Printed and bound by CPI Group (UK) Ltd, Croydon, CR0 4YY

For Anastasia and Leah

'Believe in your heart that you're meant to live a life full of passion, purpose, magic, and miracles.'
ROY T. BENNETT

Contents

Introduction: Do You Believe in Magick?   xi

Part 1:   Wicked Witches

What in the World Is WishCraft?   3

Which Witch?   9

Dispelling the Myths   15

A Word to the Wise   23

Part 2:   Magick & WishCraft

The Method in the Magick   37

The Mystic Rainbow   41

Earth, Air, Fire, Water, and Spirit   47

The Moon, the Sun, and the Stars   53

Nature Gifts and Earth Treasures   61

Magickal Signs and Symbols   65

Magickal Numbers   71

Part 3:   Prepare & Power Up

Focus Your Hocus Pocus!   81

Declutter and De-Crapify   83
Count Your Blessings   87
Forgiveness   91
Dance to Your Own Tune   95
The #MagickMonday Revolution   97

Part 4: Practical Magick
Discover Your Secret Soul Signature   103
Getting Started with Simple Spells   111

Part 5: Wishing Spells
When You Wish upon a Star   131

★ **Wishes for Lunar Magick**   **133**
Moonlight Magick Ritual   135
Menstrual Moon Magick   137
Enchanted Moon Jewelry   140

★ **Wishes for Clearing & Cleansing**   **143**
A Simple Cleansing Ritual   145
Cleansing Vibes   147
Crystal Clear   149

★ **Wishes for Power & Protection**   **153**
A Personal Power Ritual   155
Crystals of Protection   159
Increase Your Psychic Awareness   162

☾ Contents ☽

⋆ **Wishes for Midnight Magick** **165**
A Wish to Recall Your Dreams 167
A Ritual for Restful Sleep 169
Secret Starlight Wishes 171

⋆ **Wishes for Health & Wellbeing** **175**
Healing Wishes 177
A Wellbeing Wish 179
Angel Wishes Healing Spell 182

⋆ **Wishes for Money & Luck** **187**
Wishing Well Spell 189
A Magick Money Tree 191
Bee Lucky 195

⋆ **Wishes for Success & Achievement** **199**
Seeds of Success! 201
A Wish to Pass a Test 203
Superpower Success Spray 206

⋆ **Wishes for Positivity & Vitality** **211**
Positive Vibes 213
Enchanted Gingerbread Cookies 215
Vitali-Tea 218

⋆ **Wishes for Love, Sex, & Beauty** **221**
Magickal Massage Oil 223

A True Love Wish 226
The Queen of Hearts 229

★ **Wishes for Self-Care & Friendships** **233**
Self-Love Bath 235
Goddess Circle Wishing Ritual 238
Wishes of Self-Appreciation 241

★ **Wishes for Animals & the Earth** **245**
Pet Protection Wish 247
A Wish for Wildlife 249
A Seashell Spell 251

★ **Wishes for Moving On & Letting Go** **255**
A Wish for Loved Ones Lost 257
A Wish to Release Negativity 260
A Heartsease Wish 263

★ **Wishes for Sunshine & Summertime** **267**
A Pocketful of Sunshine 269
Summery Solar Tea 271
A Summer Solstice Wish 274

Afterword: Follow Your Heart 277
Resources: Something 'Wicked' This Way Comes 279
Acknowledgments 281
About the Author 283

Introduction:
Do You Believe
in Magick?

'You've always had the power, my dear.
You just had to learn it for yourself.'
GLINDA, THE WIZARD OF OZ

Have you ever closed your eyes, blown out the candles on a birthday cake, and made a wish? Did you ever toss a coin into a fountain or a wishing well? Perhaps, when you were a little girl, you sat in the garden and puffed on a dandelion, watching the seeds of your wishes float away in the breeze?

If you've ever done any of those things, then you've been practicing WishCraft. You may not have realized it consciously, but deep down somewhere in your heart you've always known that you've a magick inside you, a magick that holds the key to your power to make all of your dreams and wishes come true... in fact, we all have! But most people never get to realize the full potential of their ability to craft magick: their ability to change the world and to direct their destiny to manifest their true dreams and desires.

So that's why I've written this beginner's guide to WishCraft and magickal manifesting. When I say 'magick,' I'm referring to the magick of making good stuff happen in life, rather than the tricks a conjurer performs on stage. Through sharing the exact practices that have helped me to manifest everything – from lots of extra money to new jobs, a new man after a heartbreak, houses, vacations, new friends, and amazing opportunities (and even this book!) – I hope I'll be able to help you to do the same and manifest your desires too. Basically, I've discovered a way to make my wishes come true – and if I can do it, so can you!

But hang on a second, I hear you say. *I did all that blowing out of candles and wishing stuff when I was a kid. I wished for a pony. I wished that the cutie in the dinner queue would ask me out. I wished for a smaller butt and bigger boobs. Just this week I wished that the mortgage would get magically paid off, the car would pass the vehicle inspection, and the kids would give me five minutes peace. And how many of those wishes came true? None. Zero. Zilch. Nada.*

Honestly, let me tell you that it was exactly the same for me, too, until I discovered WishCraft. That's when I learned how to start making wishes with real focus and intent – wishes that actually manifested!

When I first started learning about magick and witchcraft, I discovered that exploring the subject as a beginner can be super daunting. Learning about witchcraft can be a bit like peeling back the layers of an onion: the more you discover, the more there is to find out. But I've found what works for me; and I know it can work for you, too. Why? Because WishCraft is easy and simple, it's powerful, and it will allow you to practice practical magick in a way that fits into your daily life.

Having worked with hundreds of women trying to make their own way in the world through micro-enterprises and multi-level marketing businesses in my career, I've come to realize that we're all very much in the same boat: we're trying to cope with all the crap that life throws at us and are left with very little space, time, or energy to take care of ourselves properly. I've spoken to and supported so many women who are trying to do everything – raise children, improve their lives and the lives of their families, get the perfect body or the perfect face, all while perpetually picking up their partner's dirty underpants off the bedroom floor – and habitually punishing themselves for not being as good at it all as they think they 'should' be every single day. Like me, and perhaps like you, too, these women have suffered panic attacks, low mood, low self-esteem, anxiety, and emotional stress. Well, enough is enough! We will pick up other people's dirty underpants no more!

Much of our innate feminine ability to focus our intentions and forge our own special spiritual pathway has been lost or forgotten in the new millennium, primarily because of the constant drains on our time and on our personal, emotional, and mental resources. When we look back at early civilizations, our ancestors celebrated both feminine and masculine energies. Pre-Christian Pagan religions worshiped male and female deities, and both women and men were honored for their unique contributions to life: creating it, surviving it, and improving it. From creation until the birth of patriarchal authority, women were worshiped for their abilities to bring forth new life, heal, and sustain their families, while men worked the land and hunted.

Today, women are expected to be the primary caregivers, excel at awesome careers, and have 'on fleek' eyebrows and false eyelashes permanently in place (at the same time as hitting the gym, drinking eight glasses of water a day, and posting the whole lot on Insta while we're at it!). Of course, we *can* and *do* successfully do all these things, but in the process we so often forget to take care of ourselves on a spiritual and emotional level. We neglect our own needs and desires in favor of supporting others, and we neglect to celebrate our own powerful place in the Universe.

WishCraft is a way for us to redress that balance. WishCraft isn't just about casting the odd spell and hoping for the best – it's an opportunity to integrate a more magickal and spiritual side of ourselves into our everyday lives. It gives us the chance to heal ourselves and our relationships. It's the epitome of 'me time,' with the added bonus of bringing to fruition our perhaps long-forgotten dreams and hopes for success, abundance, wholeness, and wellness – on our *own* terms.

WishCraft helps me to lead a life that's in tune with the natural order of the world – and with nature itself – and a life that's more in balance and harmony with my inner spirit. It inspires me to embrace the duality of the masculine and feminine energies within, and to see this reflected in the perfect harmony of these energies in nature. Through living in balance, I've learned to appreciate all the amazing things I accomplish on a daily basis – and to give myself a break! We're all doing the absolute best we can, and we should give ourselves and each other a daily pat on the back for just generally being awesome women *and* men, mothers *and* fathers, hunters *and* homemakers.

WishCraft is all about *your* reality, *your* everyday, and *your* victories – not about trying to live up to the latest glam guru's wonderful but seemingly unattainable successes. We're all too often told what 'success' means, and shown what it should look like in media, in books, and on our daily news feeds, when, of course, 'success' is a subjective concept – what makes one person happy might not be the same thing that makes you happy. WishCraft is all about you and your happiness. Whatever you dreams or goals, big or small, the WishCraft rituals in this book will help you to focus on your personal needs at any given point in your journey to living your 'best life,' as defined by you and you alone.

How many times have you heard the saying 'There's no magick formula for getting rich'? For being successful? For wellbeing, for love, or for happiness? Well, that's BS! There *is* a magick formula. Who says we can't have it all? A lot of the time, it's society telling us we can't, and quite often, sadly, we tell ourselves that our dreams are out of reach, too. The reality is that we absolutely can have it all. You can totally create the life you desire (and deserve!) without compromise *and on your own terms.* And the best bit about it is that the magick you need to make it happen is already inside you. You already have all the magickal powers you need to manifest your wishes.

WishCraft is simply the key to unlocking a door to a connection with the Universal Laws of Attraction. You can make amazing changes in your life with a little help from the Cosmos. Better yet, it's super easy and super fun. You won't need to memorize the entirety of the Major Arcana or know how the alignment of every single planet is going to affect your day – who has the time for that anyway when the kids won't eat their vegetables and your inbox has 133 unread messages?

I wanted to write this guide with a practical focus on manifesting opportunities for positive change. It's for women all over the world who, just like us, want to explore becoming a practicing witch in a way that's helpful rather than draining our time and mental resources. It breaks WishCraft down into easy-to-understand, bite-size chunks, and makes use of simple methods and powerful ingredients that can generally be found around the home. I hope this little book will help you to begin your own magickal journey; it's an exciting and enchanting one – that's for sure – and it starts right here, right now, today. You'll learn all about the secrets of tapping into your very own personal pool of magickal power – and how to become the awesome, successful, and satisfied woman you were born to be!

In Part 5, you'll find 39 WishCraft rituals to manifest everything from more money to increased psychic abilities and self-awareness. There are spells to help you with passing tests and exams; enchantments for health, wealth, and abundance; and rituals to help you call on the power of the Moon and to decipher your dreams. There are spells for better sex, a fun and easy ceremony to honor your besties in your Goddess circle (with wine!), and charms to protect your pets. There's even enchanted gingerbread. Yep, magick and cookies – yay!

Whatever you wish for, you can make it happen. I believe in your magick. I believe in you! And I'm really excited to be a part of helping you learn how to make your wishes come true and manifest your most amazing life ever! So, put on your pajamas and curl up somewhere comfy. Our magickal journey into the wonderful world of WishCraft is about to begin...

PART 1

WICKED
WITCHES

Wicked

(adjective)

3. INFORMAL

   Excellent; wonderful.

   'Sophie makes wicked cakes'

Similar: Excellent; superb; dazzling; marvelous; magnificent; exquisite; exceptional; fabulous; divine; wonderful; awesome; brilliant; badass.

Origin:

   Middle-English: probably from Old English *Wicca* 'witch.'

Oxford Dictionary of English

What in the World Is WishCraft?

'Magic exists. Who can doubt it, when there
are rainbows and wildflowers, the music of
the wind and the silence of the stars?'

NORA ROBERTS

Making wishes is very familiar to us – and something we all do all the time. Have you ever counted how many times you say 'I wish…' in a day? *I wish my hair was longer. I wish the kids would sit down and behave. I wish the Sun would come out. I wish I could afford those gorgeous designer shoes…*

If you started to count, you'd be surprised by how many wishes you make. Making a wish is simply an expression of a desire – and one which we often make without even stopping to think about, let alone to do anything about. It's for this reason that the expression of a wish alone rarely manifests anything. But when you express this desire in the form of a simple spell or ritual, the clarity and focus with which you communicate your intention and purpose to the Universe is distilled, and it becomes powerful enough to initiate subtle shifts in the Universal energy vibrations – resulting in your dreams becoming realized.

WishCraft is a very simple, pared-down form of spell-work which requires only a basic knowledge and understanding of how magick works, a few common objects you can mostly find at home, good intentions, and some positive actions on the part of the person making the wish. For the most part, WishCraft is based upon a very ancient and simple witchy art form, with a little bit of modern magickal practice thrown in for good measure. Combined together, they create a totally contemporary way of manifesting for those of us who don't have the time or resources to spend hours performing the complex rites and ceremonies that are often required of more modern witchcraft disciplines.

Witching and Wishing

I first began experimenting with WishCraft in my early 20s, after finding that the books I was reading about witchcraft and what you needed to do to become a 'real' witch were complicated and often confusing – and very time-consuming! Those witches' spells and rituals all seemed to require lots of odd and obscure articles; apparently to cast real spells (that were actually gonna work) you needed all the bells and whistles – literally! But rest assured, you don't need to stress about cardinal points, ceremonial daggers, and broomsticks to cast successful spells.

Books about witchcraft talked about joining covens, calling in the corners, and performing complex and intricate self-dedication ceremonies – and to be perfectly honest, I just didn't have the time (nor the inclination!) to wander around the woods at midnight wearing nothing but a cotton robe, wielding an elder twig or a chalice of red wine. I couldn't get to Stonehenge to celebrate the Solstices, and I didn't have the cash to splash on expensive lotions and potions. Some of the stuff I came across was super weird – weird even by witchy standards! I mean, as for where I was going to get a rusty coffin nail to insert into a pickle in order to exact revenge on a cheating boyfriend, I wasn't particularly sure I even *wanted* to know. I reckon karma probably takes care of cheating pickles eventually, anyway.

Nope. All that ceremony wasn't for me. But the books I was reading at the time made it seem that without doing this stuff, I wasn't a 'proper' witch. Pfft. I decided I liked my magick a little more chillaxed.

So I took what I'd learned and instead I started to use very basic ingredients and simple wishing rituals to focus on specific things that I wanted: a house, a new partner, a financial windfall, a new job – and it worked! It was only much later, when I discovered a book called *Wishing Well: Empowering Your Hopes and Dreams* by Patricia Telesco, that I realized what I was doing had a name.

A Bit of Cosmic Glitter and Sparkle

WishCraft has its roots firmly planted in ancient Celtic and European Pagan traditions, and over hundreds of years this simple magickal application has evolved. With the ever-increasing ease of global travel and communication, this practice has come to incorporate all the vibrancy, colors, and flavors of cross-cultural spirituality. For me, WishCraft is a combination of manifesting, meditation, and deeply focusing on my goals – with some extra Cosmic glitter and sparkle thrown into the mix for good measure! If you were to take a metaphorical cauldron and add a dash of Celtic tradition, a pinch of Western esotericism, and sprinkle a dusting of Eastern mysticism across the top, you'd be brewing a very powerful modern-day WishCraft potion!

WishCraft is an holistic, positive, and extremely effective way of realigning yourself physically and spiritually with the natural order of the Universe by working in harmony with nature and the elements and, through establishing these sacred connections, discovering and igniting the power of your personal inner goddess! Through clear insight and clarified communication with the Cosmos, followed up by conscious and positive action, WishCraft allows you to fully harness the power of the Laws of Attraction and work *with* the ever-changing tides of life, rather than against them. This deeply personal spiritual practice will allow you to ride the waves of endless abundance and opportunity, and weather the inevitable storms we all face with increased comfort and confidence. And if this sounds in any way complicated, I promise you it's not. All you need to get started are a few beautiful candles and crystals, 15 minutes of 'me time,' and an open mind.

Which Witch?

'The first time I called myself a 'Witch' was
the most magical moment of my life.'

MARGOT ADLER

WishCraft is born of a magick quite literally as old as
the hills. The emphasis of WishCraft is on practical
and simple 'Low Magick,' but this term should not be
confused with ineffectual magick. WishCraft is the magick
of the old ones: of the village wise women and herbal
healers who worked with the energies of the earth, and
who knew of and valued the power of enchanted charms,
amulets, and talismans.

So, is WishCraft the same as witchcraft then? Well, yes
and no. It's certainly a magickal practice. The difficulty here
is that, like the word 'wicked,' both 'witch' and 'witchcraft'
have changed in their etymology over time. So, in order to
answer the question, we perhaps need to consider a few
others first.

My dictionary defines a witch as being 'A woman believed to have magical powers and who uses them to harm or help other people.' It also goes on to give the informal definition: 'An ugly and unpleasant woman' (how rude!). The word 'witch' is often still used as an insult toward women – but that's a whole other chapter of a whole other book! If we ignore that, and also ignore the 'harm or help' part for a moment, essentially a witch is a woman who possesses and practices magick.

Tweaking the Strands of the Spider's Web

So the first question we should really be asking is: what exactly is magick? In *The Book of Celtic Magic: Transformative Teachings from the Cauldron of Awen*, modern-day druid Kristoffer Hughes describes magick as the energetic undercurrent of the Universe that can be used as a force to cause or create change. He explains that undercurrent as an 'energy matrix' that's accessible from the human psyche, and that can be manipulated by a magickal practitioner at their own will.

Imagine a spider's web of glistening silver that stretches beyond this world and connects all other worlds to it... Using magic[k], we tug at one strand of the web, causing vibrations to ripple from its source to affect the whole.

So if we think of WishCraft as a way of tweaking the strands of a shimmering spider's web, and manipulating the energy matrix of the Universe to our will, then, yes, in essence someone who practices WishCraft is practicing magick, and, by current dictionary definition, is therefore a witch.

Maleficent or Beneficent?

Now that we've established what magick is, the second important question we need to consider is: how can magick be used to 'harm or help' – and what has that got to do with WishCraft? Witches have been around much longer than the 'ugly and unpleasant woman' the dictionary mentions; humans have been manipulating the spider's web of the energy matrix since the dawn of time to invoke misfortune on others and to protect themselves.

During the witch trials of the Middle Ages, the widely hunted hideous hag became the definition of a witch, and her cultural clone (or Crone!) is the one that the dictionary refers to today. These women were suspected of practicing maleficent or harmful magick. In reality, the so-called witches who were persecuted and accused of using magick to do harm were more often than not just lonely old ladies and social outcasts, but back then, seeking out and ridding the world of the 'wicked women' was passed off as an essential Puritan pastime to protect the godly and the goodly.

But there was another form of magick that was also acknowledged to be in existence at that time, and another name for its practitioners. This magick is far less documented and explored – maybe because of its very nature and benevolence, and the fact that it evokes a far less grisly and gruesome archetypal witch than the one we find so fascinating. The magick I'm referring to is that of the Cunning Folk.

The Magickal Helpers and Healers

Cunning Folk were women (or men) who were spiritual members of their community and who used magick to heal and protect. Also known as folk healers, they existed in Britain from at least the 15th century until the early 20th century, when modern medicine widely began to replace the old ways of healing. In early modern times, witches were supposedly dealers in dark and demonic deeds, and Cunning Folk were what we might think of today as 'White Witches.'

These benign and benevolent witches were professional practitioners of Low Magick. They used spells and charms as part of their daily work, and were sometimes employed to combat hexes. They were also often charged with locating stolen property, finding missing people or criminals, practicing the art of divination or fortune-telling, and creating charms and enchantments to heal – they even brewed the odd love potion!

The Cunning Folk's magick was less concerned with discerning the mysteries of the Universe, and more about developing practical remedies for specific problems. These professional folk-magick practitioners experimented with what I would say is the closest definition to what could be termed as WishCraft today: they foraged and found simple and basic ingredients in order to cast uncomplicated spells for positive outcomes.

Dispelling the Myths

'For all you know, a witch may be
living next door to you right now.'

ROALD DAHL

So, we all know that real witches haven't got green faces and warty noses. They don't wear pointy hats or ride around on broomsticks either. Witches also don't have pet rats and toads and black cats, or own a collection of spiders, snakes, and bats. Okay, so I do have two pet rats. And two pet cats. But the rats are my daughter's, and our cats are tortoiseshell, not black, so that doesn't really count.

Many witches certainly do have a deep love and respect for nature and wildlife, but rest assured that you don't need to run off to your local hardware store to find a yard broom that you can convert to a Besom with twigs, and you don't need to pop into the pet shop on the way home and pick up something scaly and slithery – or spidery! Did I just hear you breathe a huge sigh of relief?

Hags, Cauldrons, and 'Black' Magick

We have Shakespeare to thank for the modern-day image of the witch. Since the first performance of *Macbeth* in the Great Hall at Hampton Court Palace in 1606, ugly hags with cauldrons have become synonymous with magickal and mysterious women. But much of the dark and creepy symbolism associated with witches in modern books and horror films misrepresents the true nature of witchcraft.

Let's take the word 'Occult,' for example. Books about witchcraft are often found in the *Occult* section of bookstores, along with other terrifying tomes adorned with demonic-looking symbols. When we think of the word 'Occult,' it tends to bring to mind all things scary and satanic. In fact, 'Occult' simply means 'hidden.' People fear what they can't see, and what they don't understand. Witches have long existed in shadowy forests and tumbledown cottages in the periphery of our minds, shrouded in mystery and secrecy; and for this reason alone, we've been both haunted and fascinated by them for centuries.

Another one of the most common misconceptions surrounding witchcraft is the notion of 'white' and 'black,' or 'good' and 'bad,' magick. There's really no such thing as white and black magick – there are only good and bad intentions. Magick itself is much more of a gray area! Using a black candle in a ritual doesn't mean that you're casting an 'evil' spell – unless you happen to have evil intentions. As you'll discover, everything you send out into the Universe comes back to you threefold, so casting magick with anything but pure intentions isn't particularly advisable.

As Halloween has become increasingly popular over the years, we've seen the modern image of the witch evolve: we've had teenage witches on TV; Quidditch-playing witches; and we've even been bewitched by beautiful enchantresses. These days, a sexy witch costume is a Halloween wardrobe staple. Practicing witches in the West are, for the most part, as commonplace now as our fascination with everything else magickal and mysterious. But it's more so the practicalities of magick that are shrouded in secrecy, and for many of us, this is part of the allure of discovering witchcraft for ourselves.

The Secrets of the Sorceress

It's my belief that as human beings we all have an innate magick within us, and this magick can be tapped into and put to good use. You'll often find in books or online, some magickal 'secret' that purportedly exists and is only discoverable once a witch has been initiated into the Craft. In reality, the secret of magick lies within the witch herself – and they may choose to use that magick in a variety of creative ways: Reiki, spiritual healing, manifesting with the Law of Attraction, oracle card reading, and clairvoyance are just a few examples. These are all ways of connecting with our psychic abilities and communicating with the spirits, the angels, and the higher powers of the Universe. In that sense, all these things could be considered as magickal.

The main difference between these types of spiritual magick and witchcraft is that witchcraft utilizes ancient magickal lore, primarily born of pre-Christian European Pagan traditions, in a specific way to affect a specific outcome – and it incorporates its own unique set of ritualistic components to make this happen.

So, are all Pagans or spiritual seekers necessarily witches? Absolutely not. What this really means is that anyone can become a witch if that's the path they choose. By tapping into our personal pool of magickal power, we can communicate our wishes to the Universe and take the actions that can bring them to fruition. And, as with anything, the more we practice, the better we become. Anyone can perform the simple magick of WishCraft – just remember that discovering the secret of WishCraft lies within first discovering the secret of our own true spiritual selves.

'Wicked' Witches of the West

Today in Western society, many modern witches subscribe to the practice of Wicca. Wicca became popularized just before the Second World War by a man named Gerald

Gardner, who claimed to be connected to a surviving ancient coven in England. Wicca has evolved from traditional ancient druid and Celtic principles, which themselves absorbed and amalgamated ideas from other magickal, philosophical, and theological concepts over time – including the ancient Egyptian, Roman, and Greek influences that later gave birth to Hermeticism, which forms the basis of Western alchemy.

Though WishCraft certainly does incorporate elements of modern-day Wiccan and Hermetic principles, the main difference between Wicca and WishCraft is that Wicca is recognized as a religion. For the most part, Wicca includes a lot more ceremonial 'High Magick' and intricate rituals involving High Priests and Priestesses.

As with most religions and spiritual pathways, there are lots of different styles and belief systems within the broad spectrum of witchcraft. Some witches are part of a coven, and some, known as Solitaries, work alone. There are many shared practices across the different disciplines: for example, practitioners of WishCraft may choose to incorporate some elements of ceremonial magick into their rituals, just as other witches may make use of simple knot magick or candle spells to craft effective wishes.

Almost all witches observe the Sabbats (the eight annual sacred magickal festivals) and pay attention to the changing seasons. They work their magick in line with the phases of the Moon and the Wheel of the Year, and have a strong sense of connection with spirits, animals, and nature. Whatever her discipline or religious beliefs, any witch who is worth her salt holds in reverence the ability to 'help' – and *never* performs magick with the intention to 'harm.' The Wiccan Rede, which is written in the form of a beautiful poem and is the declaration of the moral code of conduct that all witches should abide by, clearly defines the rules around harming none with magickal work, and WishCraft incorporates these same principles.

Any magickal practice can give a witch the tools they need to create a positive and happy life, and by focusing on simplicity and, to an extent, self-care, WishCraft does this particularly effectively. WishCraft can also be used to help others – sending out positive and loving vibes of wellbeing and healing to the Universe is as important to the practice of WishCraft as it is to any other spiritual practitioner. And each WishCraft ritual is unique to the individual witch, because it relies as much on her own will, intentions, and actions as it does on manipulating the silver spider's web.

It's for this reason that anyone can perform this magick – you don't need to be the ninth daughter of a ninth daughter, have 'Celtic blood,' or even possess any psychic gifts (that you're currently aware of!). We're all magickal, and your magick is an inherent part of you. As within and as without, as above and so below – the witch herself is part of the Universe; as much a part of the Universal energy matrix as it's a part of her!

You are the one who brings the power to your magick, and as such, you're the one in control of your hopes, your dreams, and to a large extent, your own destiny. So whether or not you choose to consider yourself to be a witch, or indeed whichever discipline of witchcraft you may already follow, you can incorporate WishCraft easily into your life and make *helpful* magick happen all around you every day!

#WickedWitches!

A Word to the Wise

'You are the most powerful tool in your
life. Use your energy, your thoughts
and your magick wisely!'

Dacha Avelin

Now that we've learned a bit about what WishCraft can do for us, we also need to understand what it *can't* do for us. Or rather, we need to be clear about the fact that while WishCraft can help you open the doors to endless, wondrous opportunities for positive change, it isn't the answer to all of life's challenges and problems – *you* are! I'm going to get real with you for a few pages, just like I had to get real with myself before I was able to change my life for the better. So read on, and trust that WishCraft will support you in every effort you make to change your life for the highest good, as long as you follow these few simple principles.

The Karmic Law and the Rule of Three

The Rule of Three suggests that whatever energy you put out there, good or bad, will come back to you threefold. Taken from the Wiccan Rede, the basic principle of any modern discipline of witchcraft is: 'An' it harm none, do what ye will,' or as long as you're not hurting anyone else, do what you like! Witches believe that every action you take causes a karmic ripple effect, just like when you drop a pebble in a pond. Positive energy creates a positive ripple, and negative energy creates negative ripples. And just as ripples get bigger as they traverse outward, so do our vibes.

It's never advisable to work with magick when you're feeling angry or upset. Even if you're casting a spell to help you overcome this, do some gentle forgiveness work or breathing exercises first so that you're in a calmer and more relaxed frame of mind. Always work your magick with the highest of intentions, and with love and positivity in your heart, and you can be sure that this love and positivity will be what the Universe sends back to you – in a big way!

Don't Cast Spells on Others

Other than with healing spells – and even then, ideally only with the other person's consent – and fun rituals created to share with existing friends and lovers, you should never

ever cast spells on other people. Let's face it, we've all been tempted to make that hot cashier at the checkout magickally fall in love with us, or to manifest a text from the ex we still carry a torch for (I've totally been there!). And who hasn't wished their current partner would be more romantic, considerate, helpful, or tidy, or look a bit more like that hot Hollywood film star we fancy?!

But karmic law, or the Rule of Three, determines that interfering with someone else's personality, feelings, or destiny is just not cool. I can hear you saying now, *Yeah, but making the hot cashier at the checkout fall in love with me isn't harmful to them or interfering with their destiny – I knew the first time I ever saw them we were meant to be married and live happily ever after!* And you may be right! But trust that the Universe knows this better than you do.

WishCraft can't make someone fall in love with you (however many love potions you buy on eBay), because interfering with someone's free will could have massive, complicated repercussions. For example, what if it turns out that your crush is a bit of an idiot who farts all the time, and you've put an everlasting love enchantment on them? Well, you made your bed, girl, so you'd have to lie in it. Literally. Forever. With an idiot. Farting. The phrase 'Be careful what you wish for because you might just get it!' springs to mind.

When crafting wishes, you should always think your wish through carefully first and consider all the possible outcomes of its manifestation. WishCraft can't and should never be used to influence another person. Even if your intention is positive, this kind of magickal meddling is still classed as 'harm.'

What WishCraft can do is help you to overcome negative vibes clinging to you from past relationships. It can also give you bags of confidence and put you in the right place at the right time to get you noticed! You can write your wish list for your perfect partner, practice WishCraft, and then the Universe will bring them to you! Honestly, it worked for me when I decided to manifest a new man after dumping my farting idiot of an ex. I got very specific, too. And when the Universe sent me my 'wish list boyfriend,' he certainly fitted the bill – even down to the funky hairstyle I'd asked for (his hair was pink), and the fact that I wanted my dream guy to have a cool hobby (he was a tattoo artist)!

So WishCraft *can* lead you to new love. It can also help you to work a little more magick into your current relationship, too, providing your partner is consenting to a bit of *Kama Sutra*-style Cosmic intervention, of course.

WishCraft can't be used to return unrequited love, but it *can* help to magickally manifest your ideal partner into your life. WishCraft can't be used to manipulate your boss into giving you a raise, but it *can* lead you to the perfect job or the perfect career advancement opportunity at the perfect time. WishCraft can't be used to make a specific person fancy you, but it can certainly be used to increase your own sexual confidence and allure... I'm sure you get the general idea. Imagine being that woman at work who just always seems to be the top pick for the latest promotion. Or that girl who walks into the room and has a handful of handsome admirers clamoring to buy her a drink. That's what WishCraft *can* do – and many, many other amazing things too!

Always Follow up with ACTION!

I'm going to give you the most honest example I can here in case you can relate: I'm quite fat. I'm not for a moment suggesting you can relate to that in particular, it's just that most of us have something about ourselves, our looks, or our bodies that we can feel insecure or uncomfortable about at times. It's also not a criticism of myself in any way; it's an honest observation – I have mirrors and I have scales! And just as an aside, who made 'fat' a dirty word anyway? Just because I'm fat (or voluptuous, curvy, or whatever other label we might prefer to put on it), it doesn't mean I'm not beautiful or that I don't love my body. I'm fat, I'm beautiful, and I love and appreciate my body. (Phew, that took me a few years to learn to say!)

I'm currently working on being a bit less fat, but that's because I'm trying to show my amazing body a bit more love and care, and be a bit more healthy so that I can live life to the fullest for longer. For years I cast spells for losing weight and buried weight-loss-aiding crystals in the ground like all the books told me to, in the hope that all my fat would magickally drain away into the soil and I'd wake up a few months later having dropped several dress sizes – and then I'd be bitterly disappointed as I sat on the sofa, munching a supersize bar of chocolate and wondering why my spell hadn't worked. Even a witch can acknowledge that sounds a bit ridiculous, right?

Here's the thing: since deciding to get serious about taking a bit more care of my body, and working on my relationship with food and self-image, I've manifested free gym passes, free fitness classes, and friendships with the two most hideous taskmasters and awesome-est cheerleaders in the whole wide world, who kick my butt with nothing but love and support every day. I've found fitness classes that I genuinely love, a gym with the most delicious pool and spa facilities that's become my second home, and whole new social circle. That's what WishCraft has helped me to do! But *I* had to go to the gym and use those free passes. I had to put in some effort too! This principle doesn't just apply to weight loss though – it pretty much applies to everything in life.

Through practicing WishCraft, you'll communicate your hopes and dreams very clearly to the Universe, and the Universe will lovingly respond to you and support you, sometimes in the most unexpected ways – then it's up to you to make the magick happen. Every wish you craft must be followed up by a real action to show to the Universe (and yourself!) that you're serious about positive change. Wishing for a new love? Do the appropriate ritual, and then arrange a night out or join a local evening class. Your new soul mate is highly unlikely to knock on your front door – and even if they did, you might be sat on the sofa in your pajamas watching TLC and having a bad hair day. Arghh!

If you want a new job, wish for it! Then update your CV – and apply for a new job! The Universe will make sure your application ends up at the top of the pile on the right person's desk, but you're the one who needs to send it out in the first instance. You won't get a promotion if you don't apply for one, however much the Universe stacks the cards in your favor.

The spells in Part 5 will help you to craft the perfect wishes and clearly tell the Universe your true intent. After each spell, there are some ideas for actions you can take to set your magick in motion. It doesn't matter what you do, as long as you *do* something. Remember that the Universe can only help you when you get real about helping yourself.

The Path of Least Resistance

When I say that the Universe can 'stack the cards in your favor,' I mean it in a metaphorical sense rather than a literal one, which brings me to two important points we always need to bear in mind when practicing WishCraft. The first is that magick will always take the path of least resistance. The second is that the Universe is incredibly literal in nature.

Let's use the subject of money as an example. Can WishCraft help you to manifest loads of money? Yes! Will that be through winning the lottery or any other high stakes gambling? Highly unlikely. Let me explain why.

Magick will always take the path of least resistance, so the Universe will always try and find the easiest route to bringing you what you want. Just like water will seep through gaps and cracks to find the quickest route to the earth, magick will take the easiest and least complicated route to granting your wishes. For this reason, ending every spell you cast with 'harm to none' ensures that your wish coming true won't negatively affect someone else. The Universe isn't malevolent. The Universe, and her magick, is neutral, and she responds to our personal energy vibrations. That's why we need to ensure that any energy vibrations we put out there, especially ones with specifically focused manifesting intent, should be positive and worked for the highest good of all.

This doesn't mean that we won't get what we want. It just means that the Universe won't take the path of least resistance by default, and in some circumstances, that can mean our wishes take a little longer to manifest while the Universe figures out a way to bring us what we want without negatively affecting or interfering with anything else – which can often produce some wonderfully surprising and unexpected results and opportunities. When this happens, trust your instincts and go with the flow. The Universe has a plan.

This is also the reason why you're highly unlikely to win the lottery, however hard you wish for it. Sorry, beautiful, but I did promise you no BS. Winning the lottery just simply isn't the path of least resistance. Think about how many people play each week, how many millions of combinations of winning numbers there are, and how many other people are wishing for the exact same win – the Universe can't help us all to win it. That's just logic. It certainly isn't the path of least resistance. In honesty, that's pretty hard work for even the Universe to engineer. Plus, winning the lottery is so random and arbitrary, that all we can do personally to affect a positive outcome is to buy a ticket.

If magick could help you win the lottery, all millionaires would be witches – and all witches would be millionaires! I'm not saying it can't happen, but gambling really isn't the best way of manifesting a magnificent and stable financial future for yourself. If you're planning on becoming a millionaire, you're far better off writing that book or putting that business plan into action. Those are things that the Universe can help you with, and that you can also have influence over yourself.

The other thing you need to consider when communicating your wishes to the Universe is the literal nature of the process. If you wish for 'more money,' and the next day you walk out and find a coin in the street, essentially the Universe has granted your wish. She interpreted your wish literally, and took the path of least resistance to bring you what you asked for. You asked for more money and the Universe gave it to you. How was she to know that what you were really asking for was enough money for a Caribbean cruise and caviar?

Conversely, if you wish to become a millionaire and you currently work at a fast-food joint (been there, done that!) you might need to work through a bit of a process before the Universe can help you achieve your final goal – upskill or go for a promotion, for example. If that's the case though, trust that the Universe will support you through each step if you keep practicing WishCraft and leveling up at each stage of your master plan (or in our case, your Mistress plan!).

Wise Words Recap

Here are the key points to keep in mind when practicing WishCraft to ensure your wishes aren't wasted:

* Don't cast magick on others unless you have their permission for healing, and never cast magick to cause harm.

* Get super specific! If you're wishing for more money, specify an amount. If you're searching for your soul mate, give the Universe something to go on. If you want a new job, tell the Universe what sort of job you'd like, how much you want to be paid, and what hours you want to work. They're called 'wish lists' for a reason!

* Make sure you always include the 'harm none' intent in all your magickal workings, and always keep in mind the karmic law of the Rule of Three.

* Wish for things you can take action to achieve – the Universe can only help us when we choose to help ourselves.

* Before crafting your wish and setting the magick in motion, give some thought to the possible ways in which your wish could manifest, ensure you're working with the highest intentions, and think about how the Universe could help you achieve it. Bear in mind the path of least resistance.

And finally...

Remember that you're deserving of abundance, and there's more than enough to go around. Be positive and embrace your right to claim your happiness and own your destiny – ask for anything you want, and never limit your dreams and desires, but do be realistic about your goals and how you might achieve them. Let's face it, if you're 93 and you've worked in a bakery all your life, your wish to become an astronaut presents the Universe with a bit of a challenge. That said, if you do want to be an astronaut then figure out a plan of what you'd need to do to get a foot in the door at NASA, practice WishCraft for each specific stage as you go along, and then go for it! With a little bit of magick, there's nothing you can't achieve if you put your mind to it!

#WitchWisdom

PART 2

MAGICK &
WISHCRAFT

'The Witch knows
nothing in this world
is supernatural. It
is all natural.'

LAURIE CABOT

The Method in
the Magick

'Magic is not a practice. It is a living,
breathing web of energy that, with our
permission, can encase our every action.'

DOROTHY MORRISON

By now I imagine that you must be wondering exactly why – and how – WishCraft works. Of course, there are some things that we can never fully explain, but as the title of this chapter suggests, there's definitely some 'method' in the magick!

We already know that, through practicing WishCraft, we can gently tug at the silver strands of the spider's web, and consciously manipulate the energy matrix to magickally manifest positive outcomes for ourselves. Essentially, when we perform a WishCraft ritual, we're creating wishes with the intention of affecting a magickal outcome, and in simple terms, we're communicating with the Cosmos. We're explicitly outlining to the Universe our hopes, dreams, and desires.

We also know that the Universe is literal and takes the path of least resistance, so it's important to pay attention to the way in which we communicate with her, as well as why we might want to. And this is where the physical components of WishCraft rituals become a little more important.

The Universe will always do her best to bring us what we want in life – we were created to be happy, positive, and productive beings that co-exist and co-create with our beautiful planet. While there will always be problems and challenges to overcome, and the circle of life by its very nature is permeated with duality – death and rebirth, joy and sadness, love and loss – we're not here to lead unhappy lives. The ups and downs of life are inevitable, but when we reach out to the Universe and tune back in to the magick that permeates everyone and everything, including ourselves, we find that we're able to live a more positive and balanced existence. We find that the Universe reaches back out to us to support us in living our lives with limitless joy and abundance, and she brings to us a wealth of love and comfort in our times of need.

For her to do this, we need to find a way to commune with her with total focus, simplicity, and clarity – and that's where WishCraft rituals and their magickal correspondences (or 'ingredients') can help. By definition WishCraft is a gentle practice that makes use of simple and natural ingredients to bring focus and clarity to our magickal communications. The more of these basic ingredients we can incorporate, the more focused our ritual will become, and the more potent and powerful the magick we muster will be.

Witches bring corresponding ingredients into their magickal practice in many ways: from practicing rituals at times that are conducive to their desired outcome (so in line with the seasons and the phases of the Moon), to working with colors, gems, crystals, herbs, spices, simple household objects, and even essential oils. Using these correspondences to focus and empower our WishCraft workings makes perfect sense.

If our energies are out of kilter with nature and our environment, it stands to reason that our lives might not always go in the direction we plan or hope for. WishCraft helps to rebalance and realign our energies with the natural rhythms of the Universe. This in turn has a positive effect on our ability to work in attuned harmony with the world.

The WishCraft rituals in this book make use of basic ingredients and easy-to-acquire items, so that you can learn to practice WishCraft successfully and develop your magickal skills and abilities in a way that's simple and fun. As you become more confident, you'll look to learn more about the different ingredients that you can use to create rituals and spells that are personal to you. But for now, in times of need, remember that even a single white tealight candle and some simple words, combined with clear, honest, and good intentions, can help you to open the channels to communication with the world around you and begin to tap into the energy of the shimmering spider's web.

The Mystic Rainbow

'Have faith in your dreams and someday your
rainbow will come shining through… if you keep
believing, the dream that you wish will come true.'

GILBERT K. CHESTERTON

When choosing colors that correspond with the intentions
of our WishCraft rituals, I look to the magick of
rainbows for inspiration. Rainbows have been celebrated as
a spiritual phenomenon for millions of years, and are woven
into the fabric of folklore and religion across the world. In
Christianity, Noah is reminded of the everlasting covenant
between God and all living creatures on Earth whenever a
rainbow appears in the clouds. In Irish folklore, if you found
the end of a rainbow, you would find Leprechauns and pots
of gold. In Polish tradition, rainbows also signified pots of
gold, but these were gifts from the angels.

In Norse mythology, 'Bifrost' is a rainbow bridge between
the earthly realm of Midgard and the spiritual realms of the

gods, Asgard. And in more modern culture, the passing of a much-loved pet is often poetically described as 'crossing the rainbow bridge.'

Many Buddhists believe the seven colors of the rainbow represent the seven continents of the Earth, and the seven colors also correspond to the seven main chakras.

The notion that there are only seven colors in the rainbow is a bit of a myth. What would be more accurate to say is that there are seven colors in the rainbow that can be seen with the human eye. There are millions of colors in a rainbow, most of which our brains are just unable to translate.

Colors are vibrational energy and reflections of light. Each color energy vibrates at a different wavelength frequency, and our eyes translate these different wavelengths in our brain to determine how a color appears. For example, an apple isn't actually red; the surface of the apple reflects the wavelengths that we 'see' as red and absorbs the rest. Black absorbs all other colors, and white reflects them all.

The WishCraft Mystic Rainbow is a spectrum of hues that correspond in their vibrational energy to specific areas of our lives – our activities and relationships, and our states of physical and spiritual wellbeing. We use this spectrum to aid us in effective communication with the Universe when we are practicing WishCraft and manifesting positive change. The WishCraft Mystic Rainbow actually contains 13 colors:

silver, white, purple, dark blue, light blue, green, yellow, orange, red, pink, brown, black, and gold.

For centuries, colors and their vibrational energies have been used in spiritual practices to align with specific intentions or outcomes, and we assign different meanings to them. Yellow, for example, might make us think of sunshine, vibrancy, warmth, and positivity. The masculine energy of the Sun promotes success, determination, and happiness. The color blue reminds us of oceans, which then have further spiritual meanings: oceans and water are linked with tranquility and wellbeing.

But it's not just the myriad colors that make rainbows so special; the atmospheric conditions need to be exactly right for rainbows to appear too. Rainbows usually occur after a storm or rain shower. They're the result of refracted sunlight hitting raindrops, which produces the optical illusion of bands of color arcing across the sky. While the Sun often shines after a rain shower, conditions aren't always perfect to produce the appearance of a rainbow.

The Magick of Colors

Witches often incorporate different colors into their magickal rituals to bring the desired vibrational energy into their practice, and to further focus their intent and strengthen the outcome of their spell-work.

The more corresponding ingredients you add to your magick, the stronger your spells become. Using a color that has a strong connection with your magickal intention helps to focus your magick more effectively because of its vibrational energy signature. Anything you can do to communicate your magickal intentions to the Universe as clearly as possible will ensure that your wish is recognized and actioned by the Cosmos in the closest alignment with your intentions.

What do you think of when you see the color red? Blood (or life)? Anger – like a red rag to a bull? Passion? Courage? Lust and sex? Love? Hearts? Our own hearts, of course, are literally red. So red works very well in rituals for passion and beauty. Green evokes the abundance of the earth: plants, trees, food, and crops, and, of course, fertility and growth. In our mundane world today, green is linked with money – so wishes for wealth and abundance are most successful when green is used within a ritual.

White is included in our WishCraft Mystic Rainbow because if you mixed all the colors of the rainbow together, white is what you would get. Isaac Newton discovered that all the colors in the spectrum are contained within white, and that they can be refracted by a prism. This is why you'll often hear witches use the term: 'When in doubt, use white,' because white contains every possible color and as such, if you're unsure of the right color to use in a spell, or you don't have the desired color to hand, white is the next best option.

We all recognize white as being a particularly spiritual color associated with peace, purity, and sanctity. All the elements associated with the 13 colors of our Mystic Rainbow (and indeed the full spectrum that we can't fully see) go into making this most magickal color of all.

These examples show how the earliest WishCraft practitioners linked colors to specific areas of life quite logically, and as our world has evolved (along with our ability to create more colors), so have our rituals, through a natural progression from those original color connections. In Part 5, you'll find corresponding colors for all the WishCraft rituals at the beginning of each chapter. I've also created a handy Magickal Correspondences Quick Reference Guide so that you can start creating your own spells and wishes too. You'll find the link in the resources at the back of the book (see page 279).

We can incorporate the vibrational energy of colors into our WishCraft workings in lots of ways, but the two most simple correspondences we can use are candles and Nature Gifts or Earth Treasures such as flowers, crystals, and gemstones. Early WishCraft practitioners would have made candles with beeswax colored with natural dyes from berries and vegetables. Unlike today, where modern coloring processes allow us to experiment with creating lots of different shades and hues, and even pretty glittery and metallic finishes, the color options would have been a little more limited back then. In pre-Christian times, our witchy ancestors would have drawn inspiration for ritual colors from the beauty and spiritual offerings of nature - the rainbow being one of the most stunning and ethereal of them all.

One thing's for sure: if you're lucky enough to see a rainbow, it's a sign from the Universe and a call to your Craft. Take a moment to meditate on the colors and see which color calls to you. Look inside your heart and you'll instinctively know what you're being told. It may be that the Universe is reminding you to proceed with your plans - or that she's listening but needs more clarification to help you, in which case you need to cast your wish with focus and intent. It may be that the Universe is calling for your help - is there a crisis or a natural disaster somewhere in the world? The Universe draws strength from our good intentions; as congregations pray for peace or comfort, witches of the world practice the Craft. Choose your colors carefully, trust your inner wisdom, and cast with good intentions whenever you are blessed with a rainbow.

Earth, Air, Fire, Water, and Spirit

'You alone are Earth, Air,
Fire, Water, and Spirit.'

DACHA AVELIN

You may remember me mentioning about witches 'calling the corners' (also known as 'invoking the elements') when they cast spells. The elements are, if you like, the angels of nature, and asking for their assistance and acknowledging them in our spell-work creates a strong connection to the powers of the Universe. The four primary elements are Earth, Fire, Air, and Water – these are the four physical entities required for life on our planet. These four elements are also linked to the Watchtowers, or the Guardians, of four cardinal points: North, East, South, and West. Calling the corners with more elaborate invocations can be an important part of ceremonial High Magick – but adding the natural power of the elements into our magickal WishCraft spells doesn't need to be complicated!

Practicing WishCraft doesn't require you to call the corners, but even in the simplest of rituals we can certainly honor the elements of Earth, Air, Fire, and Water. We can add small tokens or symbolic representations to our altars or magickal spell-casting spaces: some salt or an acorn to represent the Earth; a feather or incense to honor the element of Air; a small tealight to invite the Fire spirits to watch over us as we work; and mineral water or a pretty seashell or pearl to symbolize the element of Water.

The Elements

Some witches also believe in Elementals, or the 'spirits' of the elements. These elemental spirits were acknowledged by the Swiss physician and alchemist Paracelsus in the 16th century; he described them as Gnomes (Earth spirits), Sylphs (fairies or Air spirits), Salamanders (Fire spirits), and Undines (Water spirits). Many witches believe these Elementals carry messages to the Universe and protect us as we create our wishes.

I feel a very deep and personal connection with the Earth spirits, and I believe that in return for my small efforts to help look after the planet – picking up a bit of trash at the beach when I visit, and rescuing the odd bat – they're close to me when I'm close to nature, and when I practice WishCraft. Whatever you believe, for me honoring the elements in this simple way is an important aspect of my WishCraft rituals.

The Fifth Element

As well as the four physical elements, there's one final element – which is the most important one of all. This is the element of Spirit, also sometimes known as Aether or Ether. This fifth element represents everything: the magick of the Universe, the gods and goddesses, the magick that's within us, and the magick that's all around us.

The Spirit element and its place in WishCraft rituals is usually represented by a pillar candle – for me, it's the Goddess candle. My Goddess candle is a large white pillar candle inscribed with words and symbols significant to me. I dedicate my Goddess candle to my own sacred femininity, and to the divine female energy of Spirit; I use it to honor the Goddess (the Moon) as well as my own inner goddess! It's important to remember that Spirit is made up of both feminine and masculine energies, but as an empowered woman – and a powerful witch – I consciously choose to celebrate my own physical and spiritual connection to the Divine Feminine when I'm making magick. My Goddess candle represents Spirit, but it also represents me! You could just as easily inscribe words or symbols on your Spirit candle to honor both the divine female and male energies of the Cosmos (and yourself!) – or simply dedicate your candle to Spirit.

The Spirit Candle

The element of Spirit is all that we know, and all that we don't. It's the literal embodiment of the 'energy matrix' or the spider's web. We should always honor Spirit and ourselves as magick-makers with a Goddess candle or something that represents this higher power – that's both all around us and *within* us – whenever we're crafting our wishes.

The Moon, the Sun, and the Stars

'The dancing Sun the dancing moon the dancing stars and the dancing galaxies are the direct expression of our divine Self.'

AMIT RAY

Before the advent of modern science, our early ancestors worshiped the Moon and Sun as deities, and looked to the stars to make sense of the world around them and guide their choices. This makes perfect sense, as the cycles of the Moon and Sun define night and day, the seasons, and dark and light. The cycles of the Moon and Sun signify the ever-repeating circle of life, death, and rebirth. Long before we had electricity, modern methods of food production, and 24-hour stores, people had no choice but to live their lives by the cycles of the Moon and Sun. This inherent link with the natural balance and harmony of the Earth is still important to incorporate into our spell-work today, in order to align our magickal intentions with nature and the ancient natural order of Spirit.

In modern witchcraft, the Moon and the Sun are the physical representations of feminine and masculine energy; they're the divine couple. Their 'joining' together during the darkness of a solar eclipse reminds us that both these energies are integral to life – they can cancel each other out or they can support each other to create unity and wholeness. Like night and day – and life itself – we're a complex compendium of polarities: shade and light, bad and good, sad and happy. The Moon and Sun remind us that we must balance all aspects of ourselves to live life to its fullest in peace and harmony.

Some witches refer to the Moon and the Sun as the Goddess and the Horned God, or the Lady and Lord. Whatever our gender or sexuality, as human beings our own duality of masculine and feminine energy should be nurtured and celebrated, and this is reflected in the honoring of the Moon and Sun when we're working spells or crafting wishes. Working with lunar and solar energies when we're practicing WishCraft can help us to assimilate this divine balance, within and without. Once we've re-attuned ourselves to the natural cycles of the Moon and Sun, and we're working *with* them rather than against them, we find that it becomes easier to ride the waves of the ebb and flow of life.

The Moon

The Moon is divinely linked to femininity, psychic abilities, and unknown realms. She controls water and the tides (the lifeblood of our planet), and she's believed to influence menstrual cycles. The Moon can be considered a tripartite deity – or a Triple Goddess – represented by three discrete goddesses worshiped as one. In modern-day witchcraft, the Triple Goddess is known as the Maiden, the Mother, and the Crone (representing the Moon's Waxing, Full, and Waning phases), and in Roman mythology, she's known as Diana (the Huntress), the Moon, and the Goddess of the Underworld.

Witches understand the significance of the Moon, performing ceremonies to 'draw down' her power at Esbats, which are monthly celebrations at the Full Moon. I often have a little chat with Mrs Moon. When I take time out just to sit, light a candle, and connect with the Moon, I feel incredibly content, at ease, and reassured. It's a bit like having a cool big sister, a mother, and a wise old auntie with whom to share life's ups and downs.

Timing your WishCraft rituals according to the phases of the Moon can effect different outcomes. If you wanted to attract something with a wish (more money, for example), you would perform the ritual during the Waxing phase of the Moon: the period from the New Moon until the Full Moon. If you wanted to dispel something (negative emotions or debt, for example), you would work your wish during the

Moon's Waning phase, as she transitions from an orb back to a crescent shape.

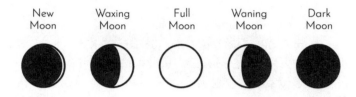

| New
Moon | Waxing
Moon | Full
Moon | Waning
Moon | Dark
Moon |

The Lunar Phases

Working lunar magick at the New Moon will bring prosperity to new projects and ventures. Lunar magick cast at the Full Moon will be especially powerful. There's also another phase between the Waning and New phases, when the Moon is not illuminated at all by the Sun and is therefore not visible in the sky. This is called the Dark Moon phase. Many witches generally don't cast magick during the Dark Moon.

The Sun

The Sun brings warmth and the growth of crops; he sustains life through the production of food to be harvested in fall. The Sun represents Fire, vitality, energy, and vibrancy. The Sun's masculine energy is associated with growth, abundance, and fertility. In modern witchcraft, the Sun is most often represented by the Stag or a Horned God, such as the Greek god Pan or the Celtic god Cernunnos. As with the Moon, the Sun God (or the Horned God) has many different representations and names spanning many cultures and religions through the ages. And, like the Moon, the Sun also waxes and wanes, but his cycle spans the year rather than a month. As it would have been in ancient times, this cycle is celebrated by witches and Neo-Pagans today during the eight Sabbats, which mark the significant solar events of the year. It's worth noting that these events may take place on different dates depending on where in the world you live.

Winter   Spring   Summer   Autumn

The Cycle of the Sun

Yule, or the Winter Solstice, is the shortest day of the year and marks the beginning of the Sun's Waxing phase as the long, dull days of winter slowly begin to lengthen into spring and summer. We should work wishes during late winter and early spring to plant the seeds of plans and projects that will come to fruition later in the year. Despite the cold, dark, and damp of the start of the Waxing phase, Mother Nature begins to awaken from her slumber, and we start to see the first signs of new life. We begin to look forward to the warmer weather: we book holidays, buy bikinis, paint our toenails... and start shaving our legs again! The Summer Solstice occurs when the Sun is closest to Earth; at this time we feel the power and heat of his strength and might the most.

Solar magick worked during the latter part of the year celebrates developments, achievements, and bountiful harvests – reaping the rewards of our hard work throughout the year. It's also a good time for clearing and decluttering by getting rid of the old to make way for the new. As the days draw in, the nights lengthen, and the world around us prepares to hibernate, treat yourself to woolly sweaters and warm cocoa; take time to reflect on the year that has passed, and your hopes and dreams for the year to come.

The Stars

Through every age, and in every culture across the world, stars have been associated with divination, portents, messages, and good luck. These days we 'thank our lucky stars,' 'wish upon a star,' and even 'have stars in our eyes'! We sing about 'catching falling stars' and recite nursery rhymes about stars that 'twinkle like diamonds in the sky.' Though much of our modern-day metaphysical associations with stars stem from the ancient Greek civilization – many star constellations are named for Greek gods – the mystical significance of stars can be traced to Celtic roots in Europe. Take, for example, the constellation Perseus, named for the Greek monster-slaying hero and son of Zeus: this constellation is also associated with the Celtic god Lugh, who dies as the nights get longer following the Summer Solstice, and is later reborn as the spring returns.

A Lucky Star

The Sun itself is a giant star. A feast in honor of the Sun and the harvest is held at the Sabbat of Lammas, or Lughnasadh; it's marked on the Celtic pictorial calendar by a bow and arrow. This festival is observed today by modern witches and is the first of the three harvest festivals of the Pagan calendar.

The Pentagram, a symbol synonymous with witchcraft, is one which we recognize as being star-shaped – so witchcraft and stars go hand in hand!

The wisdom and symbolism of the stars is inextricably linked to ancient magick. Did you know that many scientists think that gold is debris that has fallen to Earth from extinguished stars? Why would we not 'wish upon' the celestial beings that have previously blessed our planet with such beauty and riches? And shooting stars are even more synonymous with making wishes (though shooting stars are in fact not really stars at all – they're tiny particles of meteor dust that burn up in the Earth's atmosphere). Nonetheless, shooting stars are steeped in mystery and folklore; it was once widely believed that stars were peepholes in heaven that the gods could look through and watch what was happening on Earth. When the gods looked down, a star would slip and fall to Earth, and if you made a wish at that moment it would be heard by the gods, who would make it come true.

As with the Sun, the Moon, and all the wondrous phenomena that grace our skies, stars are magickal in every way – not least in their displays of endless sparkling abundance that are cast like glitter, strewn across a clear midnight-blue sky. Gaze upon the stars often, and you'll be filled with the light and awe they evoke. And if you're lucky enough to see a shooting star, remember to make a wish!

Nature Gifts and Earth Treasures

'There is magic and wonder for eyes who
know how to look with curiosity and love.'

ANSEL ADAMS

Mother Nature affords us a bountiful treasure trove of
gifts which we can often overlook or take for granted.
From the food that grows in our fields to the fish in our seas
and rivers; from our abundant fauna and flora to beautiful
gems and jewels hidden in the earth and rocks – we're truly
blessed with the wonders of this planet and all her offerings.
Herbs, for example, have long been heralded for their
magickal and healing properties and have been used for
thousands of years in tinctures and topical remedies, as well
as to add flavor and spice to our food.

Simple examples of Mother Nature's remedies include
adding mint leaves to tea to settle an upset stomach; or using

salt to cleanse a wound. Chamomile tea is a simple remedy for calming and relaxing, and a few sprigs of lavender in a pillow pouch can aid restful sleep.

Using Nature Gifts and Earth Treasures (which also include Ocean Treasures) in our WishCraft rituals connects us and our spiritual intentions to the Universe. Honoring the Universe with items collected from the environment around us enhances our relationship with nature, and this loving bond is reflected in the manifestation of our wishes.

So, what's the difference between Nature Gifts and Earth Treasures? Nature Gifts are the daily abundance of sustenance and beauty that Mother Nature affords us: foods, herbs, plants, trees, flowers, seashells, smooth pebbles, driftwood, acorns, pinecones, fallen feathers, and anything else natural that we may forage or find.

You're probably already connecting with the Nature Gifts that are bestowed on you without paying it much thought. It's widely believed around the world that to find a fallen white feather symbolizes a message from the angels, or a loved one who has transitioned. And do you remember the 'nature table' in the corner of the classroom when you were in school? Filled with fallen leaves in golds, reds, and browns; buckeye conkers and horse chestnuts; and sycamore seeds that swirl to the ground like little helicopters – the nature table is a perfect example of a Nature Gift altar, and a beautiful way to celebrate the seasons and attune to the cycle of the year. This kind of altar is a great way to mark the Sabbats, too. If you've got kids, and a little bit of space, you could set up a nature table at home and keep it updated through the year – it's a really lovely way to spend time together.

Anyone can embrace the innocent joy of noticing nature. Next time you take the dogs out, or go for a walk in the park, take a moment to remember what it felt like to be a little girl foraging for Nature Gifts. Recapture the delight you felt when you found a 'magickal' stone, a special seed, or an angel feather. Pay attention to the gifts Mother Nature sends to you – because they will have meaning and messages – and thank her for her blessings. Use Nature Gifts in your WishCraft rituals, or simply decorate your home in honor of the abundant beauty of our planet. Nature Gifts can remind you of what the Universe has communicated to you, and help you take the best decisions and actions at the right time to claim all the good that's coming your way.

In today's terms at least, Earth Treasures can be considered more valuable than Nature Gifts. This is only because nowadays we make purchases using money, and value is often measured in terms of financial worth. Earth Treasures are generally rarer or more expensive to collect and refine, but their magickal value lies more in their comparatively unique, enchanting properties. Precious metals, pearls, gemstones, crystals, and geodes have long been the markers of power, wealth, status, and beauty. They have also been long treasured and sought after for their healing and manifesting attributes. Ancient alchemists were obsessed with turning base metals into gold, and the ancient Romans would adorn their armor with precious and semi-precious gems. Stones were worn as talismans of protection, or to promote health and attract good fortune and prosperity – many of us still do this today!

Everything that sparkles and shimmers on our ocean beds, or that lies buried beneath the soil at our feet, can be considered an Earth or Ocean Treasure, as well as the precious metals that fell to the Earth like gifts from the stars themselves. Each Earth Treasure has its own unique magickal energy signature. Using these elements within our WishCraft rituals can increase the potency of our wishes, and help to clearly convey our desires to the Universe through aligning our magickal workings with the most effective energy vibrations from these naturally occurring communicators.

All the WishCraft rituals you'll find in Part 5 make use of some of the most affordable, widely available, and easily found Nature Gifts and Earth Treasures. These include common herbs, flowers, and tumbled crystals, which will all add a little extra 'oomph' to your wishes. Each Nature Gift or Earth Treasure I recommend also corresponds to the 13 colors of the Mystic Rainbow, so you can color-code your spell-casting for maximum effect!

Magickal Signs
and Symbols

'Symbols are miracles we have
recorded into language.'

S. KELLEY HARRELL

There's a myriad magickal signs and symbols that can add power to your WishCraft rituals and magickal workings – far too many to detail in this book (they would require a book of their own!). But for the purposes of beginning your journey into manifesting, here are three of the most important and commonly used symbols for any witch.

The Pentagram or Pentacle

A Pentagram or Pentacle should be used in any magickal ritual that you undertake. They're symbols of immense power and protection, bringing together all five of the elements of the nature of the Universe that we call on when we craft wishes. In its most simple form, the Pentagram is a five-pointed star. A Pentacle is the same symbol, but enclosed within a circle – this is the shape favored by witches.

The Pentacle

The Pentacle acts like a shield, warding off any negative energies around the witch, both when she works her spells, and if worn as a pendant or charm, in her everyday activities. The symbol draws all the positive and powerful spiritual energies of the five elements toward the holder. As well as the elements, the Pentacle represents the four cardinal points (North, East, South, and West) and the God and Goddess (or the duality of masculine and feminine energies, dependent upon your religious or personal beliefs). The Pentagram embodies the witch herself, with the five-pointed star representing the human form (head, arms, legs, and heart center). Enclosing the Pentagram within a circle, thus creating a Pentacle, brings all the symbolic meanings and magick together, and represents the wholeness of our connection with, and our love for, the Universe and for nature.

You can incorporate the Pentacle into your WishCraft workings in many beautiful and ornamental ways. You can wear a Pentacle as a charm or piece of jewelry; create a wooden carving or an engraved stone; inscribe the symbol into your spell and altar candles; or you can even simply draw a Pentacle on a piece of paper and decorate it with glitter and sparkles (if, like me, you're into a bit of craft and bling).

The Triple Moon

The Triple Moon, or the Goddess symbol, represents the three significant phases of the Moon: Waxing, Full, and Waning (or the Maiden, Mother, and Crone). The Moon is the Mistress of the Oceans, and so the Triple Moon symbol brings power to any water-related spell-craft.

The Triple Moon

The Triple Moon is an important symbol of femininity and divine female power, and so I incorporate this symbol into any WishCraft rituals that call specifically on the power of the Moon or feminine energies - it's especially good for spells relating to menstrual and female health. I also have this symbol inscribed into my Goddess candle to represent my own female energies and personal power, and to invoke the power and protection of the Moon in all my rituals. The Triple Moon also represents the cycle of birth, life, and death, and is a particularly good symbol to use for spells around new beginnings or releasing negativity. This symbol also makes lovely jewelry and talismans.

The Stag

The Stag, or the Horned God, invokes and honors the power of the masculine energies and the Sun.

The Horned God

He is the harbinger of life and vitality, and the Master of the Forests. Use the Stag symbol to honor him and his power in any solar rituals you perform, or any rituals for fertility, growth, success, and abundance. You can do this by inscribing this symbol into your spell candles or by placing a simple picture or Sun ornament on your altar.

Three's a Charm!

Using a combination of these three symbols (the Pentagram or Pentacle, the Triple Moon, and the Stag) on your WishCraft altar will represent all the primary forces of the Universe – and honor the duality of feminine and masculine power, as well as the ever-repeating cycle of life and nature. The two horns of the Stag and the three aspects of the Triple Moon are also reflected in the five points of the Pentagram. When used together, these three symbols reflect the wholeness of our connection and balance with the spiritual energy that permeates our lives and our existence within the Cosmos. Together, they create a potent and unified vibrational energy of power, protection, and connection.

Magickal Numbers

Numbers have been heralded for their magickal significance for eons, and their symbolism is interwoven into the tapestry of our history. For thousands of years, we've looked to mathematics and the science of numbers to understand ourselves and the world around us, make predictions, and divine sacred messages. Numbers make up the very environment around us: the Fibonacci numbers form a mathematical sequence that can be found in the biology of nature itself. For me, if there were ever a marrying of science and magick that proves the Universe was no accident, it would be the golden ratio. Daisies, pineapples, branches on trees and leaves on stems, pinecones, patterns on shells, the spiralized unfurling of a fern, and even the family tree of honeybees all share this mathematical 'code' – whereby their shape and form are based on a blueprint of a repeating ratio that the Greeks called Phi. The Universe is made up of magickal mathematics!

Numerology is one of the oldest forms of number divination and can be traced back thousands of years to the ancient civilizations of Atlantis, Babylon, Egypt, India, and Greece. The basic principle of numerology is that all numbers (and letters) vibrate to a unique frequency – just like everything else around us, numbers and letters have energy. For this reason, it's possible to use significant numbers within our magickal workings to strengthen our manipulation of the silver strands of the spider's web.

Every multiple-digit number can be reduced to a single-digit root number between 1 and 9 by adding the two digits together. For example, in numerology the number 91 reduces to the number 1 like this: 9+1=10; 1+0=1. So the numerological root value of 91 is 1.

This method applies to all numbers except 11, 22, and 33, which are considered Power Numbers or Master Numbers (or, in our case, Mistress Numbers, thank you very much!). These Power Numbers are never reduced as they vibrate at a higher frequency and embody special additional traits. Numerology can be used to help us understand the meanings of these vibrational energy frequencies and apply them to our lives. It sheds light on aspects of our personalities and demonstrates how the unique energies of the traits and characteristics encoded into our names and birth dates can influence or reveal insights about our past, present, and future. I love numerology because, if you have a lazy brain like me, it's much easier to understand and apply in a practical way than more complex divination systems such as tarot or runes.

Numbers can be incorporated into your WishCraft rituals to complement your magickal intentions in lots of ways - most rituals will include a verbal chant with a powerful reference to the magick Rule of Three. But the magickal energy of numbers can be added to your spells in many other ways, too. Numbers can be inscribed into your spell candles or you can use a certain number of petals or seeds in a spell, for example. You can even evoke the power of magickal numbers by performing your spell on a specific day of the month, or during a specific month of the year!

So, let's take a brief look at some of the most common 'magickal' numbers that witches believe to be significant.

Number 3

Of all the numbers, the number 3 is perhaps the most significant, with its principle captured in the Latin phrase *omne trium perfectum*: every set of three is complete, or anything that comes in threes is perfect. It's the number of perfection, harmony, understanding, and wisdom. It's also the first odd prime number and is therefore empowered with indivisibility. For witches, the number 3 is an incredibly powerful and significant number. It represents the witch's divine trinity (the Maiden, Mother, and Crone) and underpins the karmic law of magick – whatever you put out will return to you threefold.

The number 3 helps us to understand the principle of time: past, present, and future. Our worldview is seamlessly separated into three parts and it's with this number that we make sense of our experience and existence, and know our position and place in the world at any point in time and space. In numerology, the number 3 is symbolic of femininity, fertility, motherhood, and creativity.

Number 7

The number 7 is also considered a divine number. There are seven days in a week, and seven colors (that the human eye and brain can conceive) in a rainbow. The number 7 is the fourth prime number. There are also seven chakras corresponding to the seven levels of human consciousness. It's for this reason that the number 7 has strong links to nature, the ocean, and the earth. In numerology, the number 7 denotes spirituality, contemplativeness, and truth-seeking.

Number 9

The number 9 holds a general familiar significance to us all – cats have nine lives; when we've had a great day we're on cloud nine; and when we go for a night out, we might get dressed up to the nines. Sometimes we even go the whole nine yards! The number 9 is a particularly powerful number in witchcraft. In numerology, the number 9 is the final root number, and it signifies accomplishment, clarity, compassion, generosity, and empathy. In mathematics, the number 9 is a square number and it's the product of 3 multiplied by 3, or the sacred goddess trinity tripled. It's for this reason that we use the words 'by the power of three by three' in our WishCraft rituals – in order to give power to our words and acknowledge the karmic law that underpins our magickal workings.

Number 13

If you've always been under the impression that the number 13 was unlucky – think again! Superstitions around the number 13 are abundant and rooted in Christianity. The date of Friday 13th is considered unlucky in most Western countries because of its association with the crucifixion of Christ, and because there were 13 guests at the Last Supper. So strong is our association of bad luck with the number 13 that there are buildings with no 13th floor, hotels without a room 13, and I once lived on a street that had no house numbered 13.

As with most superstitions, we need to delve further to understand its true significance. The number 13 is linked to the sacred feminine. There are 13 lunar cycles in a year, and this is the number 13's true symbolic meaning in WishCraft. 13 is associated with female energy, psychic intuition, emotional intelligence, and the Goddess. The number 13 is made up of the digits 1 (the number of creation) and 3 (the number of sacred perfection).

The number 13 is an 'emirp' - when we reverse the digits of 13, we get the prime number 31! Prime numbers are symbolic of purity, integrity, and an incorruptible nature, and in a reversible prime number, this energy signature is particularly strong. The number 13 is also a Fibonacci prime number - this means it's a power number woven into the very fabric of the Universe and her energy undercurrents. That's why you'll find that the number 13 underpins our practical WishCraft workings, which are all centered around the 13 colors of our Mystic Rainbow and the 13 power crystals.

In fact, even this book itself is imbued with the energy and vibration of magickal numbers - and by no accident! In Part 5, you'll find 13 chapters corresponding to the 13 shades of the WishCraft Mystic Rainbow. Each of these chapters contains three magickal rituals, enchantments, or recipes. When you multiply 13 by 3, you get 39 (the magickal numbers 3 and 9); add these together and you get 12. Add 1 and 2 together and you get the numerological root value of 3 – the most magickal number of all! I designed this section to invoke as much magick as I could, so that the spells you cast from this book will be enchanted with all the positive energy I could possibly send to you... I know that you'll use it wisely, and use it well!

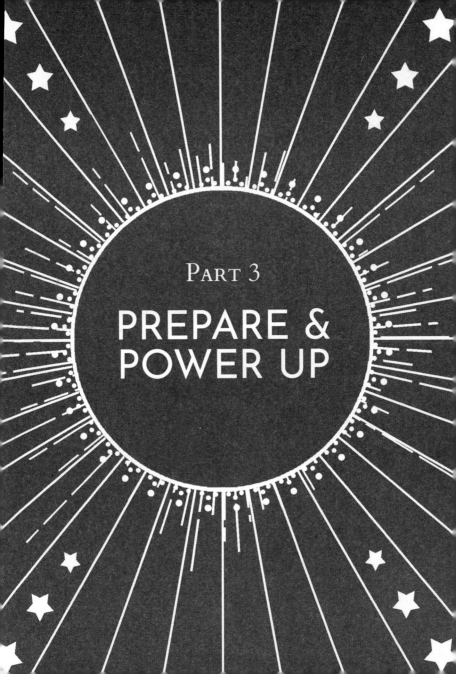

PART 3

PREPARE & POWER UP

'A great attitude does
much more than turn on
the lights in our worlds;
it seems to magically
connect us to all sorts of
serendipitous opportunities
that were somehow absent
before the change.'

EARL NIGHTINGALE

Focus Your Hocus Pocus!

'Clear focus is the mind's magic wand.'

SONIA CHOQUETTE

In order for us to make the most of our newfound magickal powers, it's important to prepare ourselves for casting really successful wishes and therefore manifesting our best lives, and to review and reflect continually upon our goals, dreams, and plans – and our successes and good fortunes! It's also just as important to acknowledge, overcome, clear, and learn from our past mistakes and hurts, which could be blocking the flow of our energy and creating unseen barriers to our desired outcomes or successes.

Power-Up Preparations are not only an important starting point to practicing WishCraft – they're also an ongoing process that will help to keep our minds and personal energy vibration clear and focused. When we do this, we maintain harmony and balance, and our magickal manifesting becomes far more productive. We also feel generally happier, healthier, and more at ease with ourselves and our lives. Sometimes this process can be incredibly pleasurable, and sometimes it can feel a little more challenging – when this is the case, trust that the Universe loves and supports you, and will provide you with everything you need to heal, move forward, and make the most of the lessons life has taught you.

In this part, I'll take you through some of the Power-Up Preparations that I practice on a regular basis, and explain how they have helped me to achieve an energetic equilibrium integral to bringing my wishes to fruition. As you develop and discover more along your own path to success with WishCraft, you'll likely find lots of helpful ways to aid this process.

Remember, we're strong attractors; magick is neutral, and so will send to us more of what we have, and what we are! The more focused and productive we are, the more clarity we will continue to achieve, and the more we will accomplish. The more abundant and grateful we are, the more we find we've got to be thankful for.

The main components I've found to be most helpful in preparing myself for positivity and powering-up my magickal practices are: forgiveness, decluttering, deep self-care, and gratitude. I find it helpful to keep a notebook or journal so that I can keep track of important self-discoveries and reflect on things I have achieved, or things I want to change.

Declutter and De-Crapify

'The first step in crafting the life you want
is to get rid of everything you don't.'

JOSHUA BECKER

Having a clear and clean physical space affords us a
clear and focused mind. When we work with focus and
clarity, our wishes are purposefully communicated to the
Cosmos.

You might like to start with clearing a special space
in your home or garden for your WishCraft practice. This
could simply be a window ledge, shelf, or coffee table. Or
you may like to dedicate an entire room to your magick.
Wherever you plan to craft your wishes, give it a tidy and
clean, and then you can perform a spiritual cleansing of your
magickal 'office' - you'll find a simple white sage cleansing

ritual in Part 5 of this book that's perfect for this! Clean and declutter your home, garden, yard, and magick-making space regularly to bring a sense of stillness, clarity, and focus to your WishCraft work, and to your daily life.

Decluttering doesn't stop at the physical space around us. We often hear the term 'digital detox,' and we all know that we really should be taking time away from our tech to focus more on friends, family, and our holistic wellbeing; calling a loved one, taking a nature walk, practicing some gentle exercise like Pilates or yoga, and, of course, performing a WishCraft ritual, are all wonderful ways of taking a break from screen time. But the online world also has some fantastic apps that can be great for practicing meditation, affirmations, journaling, health, and fitness, and we can definitely make a place for these in our lives today as long as, like with anything else, there's a balance.

De-crapifying goes one step further than a digital detox, and it's something that can make a huge impact on our overall sense of wellbeing and self-esteem. We may already declutter our inbox or clean up our hard drive (and if we don't, we really should) – not just to make our tech run faster or allow it to store more information, but because having a tidy inbox and an empty recycling bin is as important to a clear mind as a tidy office. But how often do we really look at our apps and social media and make conscious decisions about what serves us well?

Social media news feeds and stories can often be full of negativity: bad news, people's life dramas, and upsetting pictures. I'm not suggesting that we completely cut ourselves off from the world and turn a blind eye, but what does all this negativity do for our personal vibration? An infamous and rightly controversial mood experiment conducted by one of the biggest social media platforms showed that other people's moods and social media updates have a marked impact on our own mood – essentially we can obtain happy and sad emotions, and pass them on, from our social media. For a lot of us, certain aspects of social media can make us feel quite rubbish. The eternal quest for the perfect selfie has us using more and more filters, and even preferring to post pictures of ourselves as morphed mice rather than daring to share a simple natural snap. I know – I've done it! I bet you have too.

If you're finding that the pressures of social media are lowering your vibration and affecting your self-esteem (as I've experienced myself), don't be afraid to go through your platforms quietly and graciously and unfollow or disengage with anything that's negatively impacting your self-image or eating away at your positive energy. Fill your feeds with positivity and pleasantry, and your mood will improve – and so will your magick! Make decluttering and de-crapifying a regular part of your WishCraft work, and your positive vibrations are sure to enhance your ability to manifest wishes positively.

Count Your Blessings

'Magical things happen every day, if we allow it. Think of daylight, of the stars at night, a flower. A dandelion is a miracle.'

PAMELA TRAVERS

We've all been told at some point in our lives to 'count our blessings' or to 'thank our lucky stars' when we've needed a reminder that things could often be an awful lot worse. It's always been an amazing inspiration to hear stories of those who have faced extreme adversity, and who have still been able to find things to be grateful and thankful for.

It's been proven that practicing the act of gratitude has a huge and positive impact upon our mood and general wellbeing. Practicing gratitude as a daily or weekly part of our spiritual and emotional self-care has become much more widely appreciated, with celebrities from Oprah Winfrey to Tony Robbins heralding the positive benefits of simply making a journal entry or a list of everything we're grateful

★ 87 ★

for. The more we can find to be thankful for, the more abundance we feel we have. The more joyful and abundant we feel, the more joy and abundance the Universe sends to us. It really is as simple as that!

Regularly practicing gratitude has changed my outlook on life immensely – it has helped me to get through some tough times, and it has also exponentially increased my ability to manifest my wishes!

There are lots of ways to incorporate gratitude into your daily life: from a scribbling on a sticky note to keeping a beautiful journal; from downloading a simple app on your phone to leaving an anonymous note to the cleaner who makes up your hotel bed for them to find when you check out. I practice a combination of all the above and much more, but I want to share with you one of the most relaxing and spiritually moving ways that I've found to practice gratitude, so that you can give it a try for yourself and see how it helps to boost your mood (and your magick!).

** Thanking Your Lucky Stars **

On a clear evening, look to the skies and focus your mind for a few moments on the stars. If there are no clouds, you'll certainly be blessed with an abundance of stars – beautiful enough to be thankful for on their own! If I told you that you've so much goodness in your life, you could name a star after each person, thing, or opportunity that you have to be thankful for, you probably wouldn't believe me. I didn't believe it either when I first came up with the idea, but I decided to give it a try.

Start off by naming the stars for the small things you can think of: the water you drank today; the food you ate; the cashier that smiled at you at the checkout; the electricity that lights your home; the rain that watered your plants; and so on. As you focus on each star, see if you can begin to think about a bigger picture, and name even more stars for things you are grateful for: the workers at the electricity plant; the seas and oceans that bring forth rain; the flowers that bloom and bring color and beautiful fragrance to your garden, and the bees that pollinate them; the train that brought the cashier to work this morning so that she could serve you with a smile... I promise that you'll run out of evening before you run out of stars - and of things to be thankful for.

Counting my blessings and literally thanking my lucky stars is one of my favorite things to do during a Full Moon Esbat (or a Solstice or Sabbat); it's a way to show my appreciation to the Universe for all the abundance she brings to me. It also reminds me that whatever difficulties I may face, I'm infinitely blessed with things to be thankful for. So, try thanking your own lucky stars, and don't be at all surprised at how amazingly lucky you suddenly become!

Forgiveness

'Forgiveness is a gift to yourself. It frees you
from the past, past experiences, and past
relationships. It allows you to live in the
present time. When you forgive yourself
and forgive others, you are indeed free.'

LOUISE HAY

There are many wonderful books written about the power
of forgiveness, how to practice forgiveness, and how to
use forgiveness affirmations, so I'll keep this chapter brief
other than to explain why forgiveness is an important part of
preparing to cast powerful wishes.

These days we're all familiar with the concepts of being
kind to ourselves, self-love, and self-care. In the previous
chapters, we've talked about why loving and being kind
to ourselves (and to others) and practicing gratitude are
important for keeping our magickal energies positive, as this
in turn manifests more positivity in our lives. The practice

of forgiveness is equally, if not even more so, important to maintaining our manifesting vibrations, and ensuring that our witchy work is always performed with the utmost positivity and for the highest good.

The reason forgiveness helps us is because when we carry around past hurts and traumatic experiences, we create negative energy blocks that prevent us from learning, healing, and moving on. Without undertaking this process, the Universe cannot bring us what we ask for because we're subconsciously rejecting it. These subconscious energy blocks can affect every single area of our lives! From finances to relationships, friendships, fitness, health and wellbeing, our careers and productivity, and everything in between – everything is affected. How many times have we sabotaged something we wanted? A relationship, perhaps, by being overly dependent – or conversely, too reserved. A job opportunity by being late for an interview? We may tell ourselves it was because something unavoidable happened, but these are the excuses we make when we feel like life has dealt us a 'bad hand.' The Universe never deals us bad hands. The Universe gives us opportunities to learn and grow. We all face trials and tribulations in our lives. It's how we handle them and how we move forward from them that determines our future.

Forgiveness is about taking time to think around the situations where things didn't go as we wanted, and understanding our triggers that relate to past experiences we need to heal and learn from. Many of us have been through experiences that we may feel are unforgivable – me included – but it's important for us to work through these experiences and forgive because, as Louise Hay reminds us, forgiveness is a gift to ourselves. Letting go and releasing our negative energy blocks allows us to manifest more positivity, joy, and abundance in our lives. Practicing forgiveness on a regular basis ensures that we're always moving forward, and never left lingering in the past.

As important as it is to forgive a person or experience that has impacted us, it's equally as important to forgive ourselves. We're often our own worst critics, and our own worst enemies! Being kind to ourselves and raising our signature energy vibration relies upon us accepting and acknowledging our faults and flaws and our inherent fallibility as human beings – and then forgiving ourselves, and giving ourselves permission to feel worthy, to feel deserving, and to lead the happy and abundant lives we're meant to. This is when we find that our magickal manifesting becomes surprisingly powerful.

You don't need to perform a full ritual to practice forgiveness, though I have included a couple of my favorites in Part 5 for you to try. Most of the time, I simply light my favorite candle and spend 10 minutes jotting in my journal to go through the following steps:

* What or who is the person or event that's causing me pain or anger?

* What are the feelings, fears, or other emotions that thinking about this person or event brings up for me?

* What aspects of this person or event do I need to forgive in order to move forward?

* What affirmations, words, or thoughts can I use to achieve this?

Exploring issues and memories around your triggers and energy blocks, and then practicing forgiveness to release them, is an ongoing process. Sometimes it can be challenging, too, but trust that for every experience, person, or action you forgive, you've opened up a part of your heart to receiving something wonderful and good.

Dance to Your Own Tune

'Music acts like a magic key, to which
the most tightly closed heart opens.'

MARIA AUGUSTA VON TRAPP

As we now know, practical magick is all about energy. The energy we create, the energy we put out there, and the energy we 'tweak' when we cast our WishCraft spells. We also know that the more positive our personal energy, the more positive the outcomes of playing with the energy of the Universe will be.

One of the easiest and most successful ways a witch can raise energy and raise her vibration is to sing and dance. Music has a huge impact on our emotional vibration: sad songs can make us feel down, happy songs uplift us, music can soothe and relax us, and certain songs have the power to manifest memories and recapture moments of our lives from years earlier. In a nutshell, music is powerful. That's why witches often incorporate music into their spell-work.

Traditionally this was done through chanting and even drumming (you'll have heard the phrase 'drumming up enthusiasm,' for example). When we chant and dance or sing to a beat, it raises energy. This energy then serves to fuel our magickal fires. These days though, chances are that the neighbors won't particularly appreciate us wassailing out of the windows at the Full Moon or banging about on a bass drum at midnight. So, unless you happen to live in a detached house in the middle of nowhere, you may just want to tune in to your favorite playlist instead.

Music can be used during WishCraft rituals to raise your energy or to relax. You can also make your magick more effective by listening to music and raising your own vibration as often as you can in your daily life: when you're doing the housework; when you're in the car, at the gym, or even out shopping with your earphones in. Music has the power to make us feel good. And it's when we feel good that our magick is at its most powerful.

The #MagickMonday Revolution

'It's not enough to just survive something…
that's not the point of life. You've got
to thrive. You've got to feel happy.'

MEGHAN, DUCHESS OF SUSSEX

Have you noticed that these days, everything about Mondays is 'motivational'? As soon as we start scrolling through social media on a Monday morning, the same tired old memes start popping up: 'New Week, New Goals,' 'Get Your Game Face On,' 'Show Up, Stand Out,' and on it goes.

I don't know about you, but I feel about as motivated as a mollusk on Mondays. Let's be honest, Mondays are completely crap. It's either the early morning run for the bus, which you miss because you laddered your tights after you slept through your alarm; or the dreaded backlog of emails in your inbox; or (my personal favorite) the disapproving eye of the school secretary when you finally get the kids out of the house, find a parking space, and realize you've forgotten to grab their lunch or gym kit or their art project or drama costume. You know the one – the look that says: *All the other mothers managed to remember everything. Why didn't you get it ready the night before like all the other normal, super organized parents?*

Now, don't get me wrong here, motivation is definitely important when we're setting out to become a Wickedly Successful Woman with WishCraft, but I personally believe that there's a time and a place for it – and in my opinion, that's not a Monday morning! I honestly believe that the only people pretending to be motivated on Mondays are those that need to motivate others to make them money.

From now, we're going change 'Motivational Mondays' to 'Magickal Mondays.' I know that you'll still have the assault course of the commute or the scary school run to contend with, but I want you to make a pact with me right now that you'll find time, even if it's just a few moments, to do something for yourself on a Monday! It can be a WishCraft ritual, a relaxing bubble bath, a mini-meditation, coffee with a friend, a quiet five minutes to read your favorite book or watch a guilty pleasure TV show – it can literally be anything, as long as it's something that makes you feel good.

Why? Because the more time you take back for yourself in this mad world, the more amazing you start to feel. Focusing on self-care refreshes and invigorates us. When you make time for yourself, you find that you become happier in the here and now.

The Universe brings us more of what we already have, so by taking time out to relax and take care of ourselves, we attract more ways to find small moments of joy and pleasure in our daily lives. The more we bring balance and harmony to our lives, the more powerful our magick becomes!

So, you and I are going to start a revolution with women all over the world like us, and take not-so 'motivational' Mondays – and make them magickal! Put your left hand on your heart and say this together with me right now:

I pledge to make time for myself
on magickal Mondays!

I believe you, so let's do this. The revolution starts with you!

#MagickMonday

PART 4

PRACTICAL MAGICK

'Always throw spilled salt
over your left shoulder.
Keep rosemary by
your garden gate. Add
pepper to your mashed
potatoes. Plant roses and
lavender, for luck.'

ALICE HOFFMAN

Discover Your
Secret Soul Signature

'There are cultures in which it is believed that a
name contains all a person's mystical power.'

DIANE SETTERFIELD

Let's move on to exploring the more practical aspects of WishCraft and how to build it into your daily life. Firstly, I want to tell you about your secret soul signature, or your secret 'magickal name.' Words and names have power for witches. Some even believe that just talking ill of someone using their regular name acts as a sort of 'hex' or curse. It's certainly not unusual for witches to use a magickal name, and chances are you wouldn't know if they did; most witches keep their magickal name a secret for protection when they're working their spells.

Now, I'm not entirely sure that I believe someone can hex me just by gossiping about me and using my name, but I do love the fact that having a secret magickal name gives me a private and totally personal identity to use when I commune with the Universe. It also helps me to distinguish my magickal self from my everyday persona. Having a secret magickal name that I work with helps me to detach from the hubbub of my more mundane life, and fully immerse myself in the magickal and the mystical.

Witches who use a secret magickal name will generally only do so during rituals, ceremonies, and other magickal workings, and only they, or those within their coven (if they have one), will know it. Magickal names can be anything, and witches often draw inspiration from nature or celestial entities. Once you have a magickal name, you can integrate it into your spiritual practice in lots of ways to deepen your connection with the Cosmos. For example, I have my magickal name inscribed on my Goddess candle along with the Triple Moon symbol.

A Method for Discovering Your Secret Soul Signature

Discovering your magickal name is fun and can reveal some of the magickal skills and abilities that you may not have realized you possess – so I thought I'd share with you the method I used to divine my secret name. I love this method because it uses numerology to decode a special number that corresponds to a magickal name. Your magickal number and name possess a unique energy signature that uncovers the secret nature of your inner witch! Through using numerology to help divine your magickal name, you'll decipher the hidden energy signature that the Universe intended for you, and the one you'll carry through all your lifetimes and reincarnations. It's the secret name of your soul!

When I was choosing my magickal name, I wanted to celebrate Mother Earth's generosity, and ensure that the name I worked with had a deep and meaningful connection to nature and the planet. So, in this method, the magickal names are inspired by Earth Treasures. Earth Treasures are all around us: from precious metals bestowed on us by the stars, to crystals, geodes, and gemstones, and even to exquisite underwater jewels like pearls and pretty corals. When it comes to magick, they're not only extremely beautiful but incredibly powerful too! Combining the vibrational energy of your magickal number with an Earth Treasure that resonates at the same numerological frequency ensures your magickal name vibrates with your unique personal energy signature, revealing even more about your magickal self, and honoring your purpose and destiny as a witch.

To discover your magickal number, we're going to combine the two most important elements of your numerology chart: your Life Path Number (based on your date of birth) and your Destiny Number (based on the numerological value of the letters of your name). Your Life Path and Destiny Numbers are important because they determine your life purpose and the destiny that will fulfill you. Once you've worked this out, you can cross-reference your magickal number with the corresponding Earth Treasure to discover your secret magickal name. This method is super easy to do (even I managed it!) and you can use the tables below to help you.

★ Calculating Your Magickal Name ★

Tip
In basic numerology, every multiple-digit number can be reduced to a single digit root number between 1 and 9. The only exception to this are the numbers 11, 22, and 33; they're considered Power Numbers and should never be reduced.

Your Life Path Number
To start, first work out the root number of your date of birth to determine your Life Path Number like this:

Say, for example, your date of birth is 27 August 1989.

If you live in the UK or Australia, your date will probably look like this: 27/08/1989.

If you live in the US, your date will probably look like this: 08/27/1989.

It doesn't matter too much, as long as the numbers are the same.

2 + 7 + 0 + 8 + 1 + 9 + 8 + 9 = 44

4 + 4 = **8**

So, the number 8 would be your Life Path Number.

Your Destiny Number

Then you need to find out your Destiny Number. You work this out using the corresponding numbers to each letter of your name, as in the table below:

1	2	3	4	5	6	7	8	9
A	B	C	D	E	F	G	H	I
J	K	L	M	N	O	P	Q	R
S	T	U	V	W	X	Y	Z	

Tip

Use ALL names, including any middle names, spelled exactly as they are on your birth certificate and in full. Even if you've changed your name, only your original name that you were given at birth will give you your Destiny Number.

So, if your name is Jade Susan Jones, you would work out your Destiny Number using the table below like this:

J A D E

1 + 1 + 4 + 5 = **11**

S U S A N

1 + 3 + 1 + 1 + 5 = **11**

J O N E S

1 + 6 + 5 + 5 + 1 = 18 = 1 + 8 = **9**

Remember, 11 is a Power Number, so you don't want to reduce it. If you don't find a Power Number in your name, you should keep reducing the numbers until they each reach a single digit.

As Jade does have a Power Number, she wouldn't reduce it further – instead she would add together the three numbers, and then reduce them down again until she reaches a single digit (unless you come across another Power Number!) like this:

11 + 11 + 9 = 31

3 + 1 = 4

So, the root number of the name Jade Susan Jones is 4, and that's Jade's Destiny Number.

Your Magickal Number

Finally, you need to combine your Life Path Number with your Destiny Number, so simply add them together like this:

$8 + 4 = 12$

$1 + 2 = 3$

So, the number 3 would be Jade's magickal number!

Your Magickal Name

The table of Earth Treasure names below have all been calculated using their numerological values, making them extra revealing. Each name is imbued with unique magickal and healing properties.

Using your magickal number, connect your corresponding personal energy signature to your magickal name and the Earth Treasure it represents.

1. Angel (Angelite)

2. Gilda (Gold)

3. Amethyst

4. Emerald

5. Heliodor

6. Peridot

7. Pearl

8. Opal

9. Chalcedony

11. Sapphire

22. Coral

33. Aurora (Auralite)

Jade's magickal number (3) reveals qualities of creativity, artistic talent, joyfulness, and self-expression (among many more). The Earth Treasure that forms her magickal name, Amethyst, reveals her abilities to dispel anger and rage, balance mood swings, and alleviate sadness and grief. Amethyst is also used for spiritual awareness and enhancing psychic abilities. So, Jade is a born entertainer with the ability to heal and counsel. She's also highly intuitive and has psychic abilities waiting to be discovered or further developed.

Combining your numerological energy vibration with a corresponding Earth Treasure to divine your magickal name reveals your unique hidden strengths and talents. You can use this knowledge when crafting wishes to define and enhance your magickal goals and outcomes. And I can't think of anything as lovely as being able to choose a beautiful piece of jewelry or a crystal that corresponds to your Earth Treasure as a constant reminder of your very personal connection to the Cosmos.

So, whether you choose to keep your newly discovered magickal name a secret or share it with the world, be sure to check out the resources page at the back of this book (see page 279) where you'll find the link to download and print your own secret soul signature profile for free - you may be surprised at what it reveals about your inner witch!

Getting Started with Simple Spells

'Witchcraft is about taking the raw,
beautiful, and powerful forces of our world
and using them to create change.'

TONYA A. BROWN

Performing a WishCraft ritual doesn't require many physical items at all, but most witches do like to create a special magickal space to work their spells, usually in the form of an altar.

A dedicated altar allows you to honor the important elements and ingredients that will help make your wishes come true, and gives you the physical and mental space to prepare to cast very powerful magick. Before using your magickal space to make wishes, it's always advisable to perform a simple cleansing ritual to clear your environment of any negative energy and ensure that the vibrations around you are positive and pure.

Creating a Simple Wishing Altar

For a basic WishCraft altar, you'll need:

* an altar space (such as a coffee table or window ledge)

* a white pillar candle (your Goddess candle)

* white sage incense sticks or cones; or a white feather (Air)

* a white, unscented tealight (Fire)

* a small dish or bottle of spring, river, or ocean water; or a seashell or pearl (Water)

* a small dish or bottle of salt; or an acorn (Earth)

* suitable candle plates or candle holders

* a suitable ash-catcher or incense cone holder

* a Pentacle (charm or picture)

* a bodkin (a blunt sewing needle) or craft knife to inscribe you candles with your magickal goals

* lunar and solar energy symbols – small ornaments or pictures of the Triple Moon and Stag, or gold and silver candles*

* a pretty white or purple altar cloth*

* Optional

A Simple Table Altar

Coffee Table Altar

Coffee tables are perfect for crafting simple WishCraft spells and rituals, though any small table works well. It doesn't matter what shape it is – you just need enough room to set out your candles and spell ingredients. If you like, you can cover it with a pretty cloth to protect it while you work and make your magick altar look even more special. You can even use a small patio table if you prefer to work outside.

Window Ledge Altar

Window ledge altars are perfect if you only have a small space at home, and they can be especially nice for more permanent setups. My bedroom windowsill is home to a WishCraft altar, and I love having this space readily available for rituals if I don't have much time or if I want to do something decorative to celebrate the changing of the seasons. If you don't have a suitable windowsill, a spare shelf or even a mantelpiece works just as well.

A Simple Window Ledge Altar

Using Candles

Safety First

Always use a suitable candle plate and a candle holder. You can use sticky tack or a few drops of melted wax to keep small candles extra secure in their holders as you work your spells. Never leave a lit candle unattended, and when setting up window ledge altars, be careful to keep flames away from curtains or other soft furnishings. It's not advisable to work with lighted candles when you're tired or have been drinking alcohol, and always be sure to keep candles away from curious pets and children. The same goes for incense sticks and cones.

Spell Candles

Choose a colored spell candle conducive to your magickal goal. Spell candles or chime candles are great for this purpose as they're small and burn for the perfect time to cast a simple spell, but you can also use dinner candles and votive candles, too. Avoid scented candles unless the fragrance is one that's conducive to your magickal outcome, or the spell calls for them. In an ideal world, beeswax candles should be used for all magickal-related stuff, as they're natural and certainly would have been the only choice for our ancestral witchy sisters. That said, they can be a little more expensive and not quite so easy to come by, so don't worry if that's not an option for you.

Tealight Candles

Tealights are very versatile and you should have at least one white tealight candle to represent the element of Fire when you set out your altar.

Pillar Candles

You'll need a plain white pillar candle or Goddess candle for your altar. Colored pillar candles are generally too large to use for most spell-work (unless you happen to be performing a massive ceremonial ritual), and candles should only be used once for each spell, so don't spend lots of money on big, fancy candles. The only exception would be silver and gold pillar candles for the solar and lunar rituals you'll find in Part 5, or for rituals that require the candle to be alight and burning over a significant period of time when you begin to practice more advanced WishCraft. For most rituals, and certainly all the ones in this book, smaller candles are absolutely fine.

Inscribing Candles

Inscribing candles imbues them with the power of the energy of the person, thing, action, or emotion you're aiming to attract or dispel with your enchantments. You can inscribe a candle with your magickal name, with something you wish to attract like 'Love' or 'Money,' or with something you want to dispel such as 'Debt' or 'Anxiety.' It also helps you to focus your mind and your intentions as you cast your spells. Inscribing your candles can be done (carefully) with a needle (a blunt bodkin needle used for sewing or knitting is best) or a craft knife. The direction in which you inscribe your candles is important:

★ To attract something, you should inscribe your candle from wick to end. This symbolizes the action of 'pulling' something toward you.

★ To repel something, you should inscribe your candle from end to wick. This symbolizes the action of 'pushing' or sending something away.

Anointing and Dressing Candles

Anointing your candles with oils and dressing them with herbs is another way of empowering them with magickal properties and energies, and clearly expressing your will and intentions to the Universe when you craft your wishes. Again, the way in which you apply oils to your candles is significant:

★ Place a few drops of the oil you wish to use in a small, shallow dish.

✻   Dab your fingertip in the oil and apply it to the candle thinly all the way around.

✻   To imbue the candle with the powers of attraction, work from wick to end.

✻   To empower the candle to repel, work from end to wick.

To dress your anointed candles with herbs or petals, scatter the ones that correspond with your spell on a piece of paper and simply roll the candle across the page, place it in its holder ready to light, and cast your wish. The remaining herbs can be added to charm bags, while some spells call for a pinch to be scattered (from a height so as not to burn yourself) over the flame.

Using Incense and Essential Oils

Incense

Incense comes in lots of different forms, from joss sticks to cones, and even grains, powders, and resins. For crafting wishes, premade joss sticks and incense cones are the easiest and cheapest to find, and they work perfectly. For a standard altar, a stick or cone of white sage incense works well to represent the element of Air, and it's widely used for its cleansing and purification properties. You can find lots of different fragrances of incense (I personally avoid pre-blended 'luck,' 'love,' and 'money' incenses and opt for a specific fragrance to be sure I know exactly what is going into my spell!), and although they're generally optional, they can certainly add extra flavor and focus to your WishCraft rituals. When using incense sticks or cones, you'll need a small ash catcher or cone holder.

Essential Oils

Essential oils bring corresponding powers and focus to your enchantments in WishCraft rituals. They can be used to enhance potions and spell pouches, and to anoint candles and crystals too. Essential oils can be very strong, so take care not to spill them; store them carefully, follow the manufacturer's instructions, and don't use them if you suffer with allergies. If you're adding them to oil blends to be used on the skin, be sure to dilute them with an appropriate carrier oil such as grapeseed or sweet almond oil, and perform a patch test to be on the safe side.

Spell Bags and Pouches

Many WishCraft spells call for a small spell bag. Spell bags can be easily and cheaply acquired online or from your local MBS store, and come in a variety of pretty colors and fabrics. If you're a little bit crafty and like to recycle (and you have a few minutes to spare), you can even make your own spell bag by simply cutting a small oblong of old fabric about 2in (5cm) by 4in (10cm), folding it in half, and stitching the two edges to make a pocket. Once you've added your ingredients to your spell bag, just gather and tie the open edge with an appropriately colored ribbon.

Using Herbs, Spices, and Flowers

Some of the rituals in this book require herbs, spices, or flowers, all of which you'll most likely find in your store cupboard or your own garden. Both fresh and dried varieties of either work well. Any which you don't already have you'll be able to find easily and inexpensively in a local store. But don't worry too much if you don't have every single element of a 'recipe' – the ingredients help to focus your intent and communicate it to the Universe, but most of the magick is in the power of your own visualizations, words, and actions.

Using Crystals and Tumblestones

Crystals, geodes, and tumblestones are not only beautiful, they're also incredibly powerful when it comes to magick and anything metaphysical. If you're particularly interested in crystals and their healing properties, then there are hundreds of books to be found on the subject. To keep things simple, the WishCraft rituals in this book make use of just 13 of the most common and easy-to-acquire crystals, selected to complement the energies of each wish you cast. These beautiful little Earth Treasures can be charged with magickal energy and kept in spell bags, in your pocket, or placed around your home.

Whenever you get a new crystal, you should cleanse it by immersing it in running water or leaving it out in the rain. Once its energies are purified, you should charge it by leaving it on a windowsill or outside in the moonlight overnight. Crystals can also be charged with sunlight, but check first as some can be damaged by the Sun. You can also place your crystals on a Pentacle symbol to charge them. Cleanse and recharge your crystals regularly to keep their energy vibrations optimal. You can then 'imprint' a magickal purpose on your crystal when you use it in a WishCraft ritual.

Ribbons, Strings, and a Few Other Things!

A couple of the rituals require colored ribbons or thread, easily found at your local craft store. And whenever you take a nature walk, remember to collect any gifts that Mother Nature leaves for you to find – pinecones, seeds, acorns, feathers, pebbles, and seashells are all around us in abundance and will be useful for your WishCraft spells.

Just a little note from Mother Nature: please don't pick wild or rare flowers, don't use or consume any herbs or plants if you're not sure exactly what they are, and *never* disturb any wild habitats. Finally, in recent years geologists have asked the public not to take too many trinkets and treasures home from the beach, for fear that collecting rocks and shells could damage the coastlines. It goes without saying that if you're lucky enough to live near to, or visit, an ocean that contains coral, please don't touch or in any way damage this vital marine habitat. Be careful and considerate of the environment whenever you are collecting Nature Gifts for your rituals, don't take anything that's living (other than common garden plants), and never take more than you need. In return, the Elementals will be careful and considerate with your wishes.

Witch Way Round?

Directions are significant in any form of witchcraft. The cardinal points of North, East, South, and West are important, as are the ways you perform certain actions – such as anointing a candle downward to manifest, or upward to dispel. But equally as important are the directions in which you may spin a charm around a candle flame to enchant it, or how you cast a magickal circle of protection.

The two directions you'll use when casting wishes are either clockwise (to attract), or counterclockwise (to repel). The witchy terms for these directions come from the ancient Scottish Gaelic language: clockwise being *deosil* (or sunwise), meaning to turn from East to West following the direction of the Sun – considered to be the 'correct' or prosperous course. Counterclockwise is known by witches as *widdershins* (or lefthandwise), essentially meaning to go the wrong way, and is used to 'unwind' or 'undo' something, or to release something negative.

The Magick Circle

I don't mean the secret club that magicians belong to. I'm talking about a witch's magick circle of protection. Which is a real thing – even though you can't see it. It's a bit like an energy forcefield that wards off negativity. If that sounds like a bit of a weird concept, think about it like this: we can't see love, but we know it exists because we can *feel* it. Magick circles are exactly the same. We can't necessarily see them, but we can feel them, so we know that they're there.

When working with the Universal energy forces, it's important to cast a circle to create a pure and clear environment in which to communicate with the Cosmos. Traditionally, witches would literally 'sweep' their circle with a broom or Besom, but you can just as easily create your circle using visualization.

⋆⋆ Casting a Circle ⋆⋆

Simply stand in front of your altar, and imagine a bright white light filling your heart.

1. Next, point your left finger and imagine this white light traveling down your arm and out through your fingertip, like a steady stream of white lightning, or a glowing beam.

2. Turn deosil (clockwise) and visualize this steady beam of lovely white light creating a circle around you and your sacred space.

3. As you join the circle together, imagine this protective light completely enveloping you and your altar - from all sides and all directions, above and below, as though you're standing in a beautiful ball of glowing, pure energy. Your circle is now cast, and you're safe and protected with positive vibrations.

Once you've cast your magick circle, you're ready to begin your WishCraft work. And once you've finished, it's just as important to close your circle so that you and your spell remain purified and protected from any other external influences. To do this, simply point your left finger again, and imagine your white light being drawn back into your fingertip, through your arm, and back into your heart as you make one full turn widdershins (counterclockwise).

Once you're facing your altar again and your circle is closed, you need to allow any remaining magickal energy clinging to you to be returned to the earth to do good, and recenter and rebalance your own energies – we witches call this grounding.

Grounding

Grounding could be considered a little bit like 'earthing' a human being, in much the same way as we might earth an electrical current. Magickal energy can cling to a witch after she has been magick-making, and we need to allow this energy to be released so that we can return to everyday tasks. Plus, a few positive magickal vibes are very good for the Earth.

There are several ways to ground yourself after spell-casting. If you're outside, you can lay your hands on a tree or on the earth itself. If you're indoors, you can simply sit or lie for a few moments on the floor, relax, and allow any leftover sparkles to drain back into the ground. Simply pause for a few moments, connect with something rooted in the earth, take a few deep breaths, and recenter yourself. It's as easy as that.

★ Seven Simple Steps for ★ Crafting Awesome Wishes

Now that you've learned a little bit about how WishCraft works, and you've understood some of the basic principles that are used by witches to make magick, and you've gathered your basic ingredients – you're ready to start casting your first spells and making your wishes come true! So here are the basic steps you need to perform a simple but successful WishCraft ritual:

1. Gather your ingredients and set out your WishCraft altar (if required for the ritual you are performing).

2. Focus and relax. If you are incorporating music into your ritual, set your preferred playlist to an ambient volume. Perhaps dim the lights and make sure your sacred space is comfortable and free of all distractions.

3. Cast your circle.

4. Light your Goddess or Spirit candle, your Air incense (if using), and your Fire tealight. Take a few deep and soothing breaths, and then perform your ritual.

5. At the end of your ritual, thank the Universe and any spirits you've called upon for assistance. Extinguish your altar candles safely and close your magick circle.

6. Ground yourself and, if possible, open a window or take a few moments outside to release your magick and recenter yourself.

7. Follow up with positive action!

Part 5

WISHING
SPELLS

'The moon has awoken
with the sleep of the sun.
The light has been broken,
the spell has begun.'

MIDGARD MORNINGSTAR

When You Wish upon a Star

'Sometimes while gazing at the night's
sky, I imagine stars looking down making
wishes on the brightest of us.'

RICHELLE E. GOODRICH

Now that you know a little bit about magick and how WishCraft works, it's time to give it a try for yourself! This section contains 39 of my favorite wishing spells. Some are really simple, and some are slightly more advanced – but all are very easy to do! Most of the spells call for setting up your WishCraft altar, but there are also some that don't require anything more than a bit of 'me time.' You'll find a super relaxing self-love bath, recipes for baking enchanted cookies, and even a ritual based around brewing a simple cup of herbal Vitali-tea! These unfussy and fun spells can be integrated into your daily life for some added sparkle, so that as you work on the more specific manifesting spells, you'll be 'powered up' with happy vibes, keeping your own energy fresh and attracting all the good that you desire – and deserve!

Each of the chapters in Part 5 corresponds to the 13 power colors of our WishCraft Mystic Rainbow, and in the introduction to each chapter you'll find a summary of the main magickal correspondences for the wishes contained within. Different sources all vary in their recommendations for the most conducive spell ingredients to manifest a specific wish, but the ones I've selected for these rituals are those that I've tried and tested myself over the last 20 years – and they've certainly worked for me.

Don't worry if you don't have a specific item for a spell. Work with what you have or substitute the item for what feels meaningful for you. Remember that the true power of the wishes you cast is in your heart and in your intentions – and in the positive actions that follow!

WISHES FOR
LUNAR MAGICK

'Connecting with the Moon reconnects us with the
Divine – with our Divine selves and with the Cosmos.'

YASMIN BOLAND

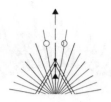

Magickal Correspondences

Key words:	Femininity; divinity
Color:	Silver
Earth Treasure:	Moonstone
Nature Gift:	Driftwood
Herb or spice:	Fennel seeds
Flower or plant:	Moonflower
Incense:	Jasmine
Essential oil:	Coconut

⋆★ Moonlight Magick Ritual ★⋆

Purpose

This incredibly simple but effective all-purpose ritual can aid your other magickal workings by creating a strong connection with the Moon and drawing down her power. It's lovely to perform this ritual outside under the light of a Full Moon on a balmy summer's eve, but if it's freezing and raining (if you live somewhere like me, it usually will be), setting your altar up on a windowsill will do just fine!

Lunar Phase

Full Moon

Ingredients

~ Silver spell candle

~ Moonstone tumblestone

~ Silver spell bag

Method

1. Set your altar and cast your magick circle.

2. Light the silver spell candle and pass your moonstone around it three times deosil.

3. Raise both your arms high above your head with your palms up toward the Moon, and send her this prayer:

> *Maiden Moon, please share with me*
> *All your flight and energy.*
> *Mother Moon, please send to me*
> *All the magick that I seek.*
> *Waning Crone, please show to me*
> *All the wisdom that you see!*
> *I use your strength for highest good*
> *And all is known and understood.*
> *By the power of three by three,*
> *I invoke thee into me.*

4. Meditate for a while on the Moon's light and beauty, and feel your connection with her deepen.

5. When you feel ready, gently blow out the candle and say:

> *I wish it, and so it is!*

6. Close your magick circle and remember to ground yourself.

7. Leave your moonstone to charge by the light of the Moon's beautiful energy - overnight on a window ledge or outside if the weather is fine.

8. Once your moonstone is imbued with the Moon's power, pop it in a silver spell bag and keep it safe.

Action

Meditate with your magickal moonstone often, and place it on your altar near your Goddess candle to invoke the Moon's knowledge and wisdom when you work your magick. Once a month, cleanse and recharge your moonstone with this spell to 'top up' its magickal moonlight energy.

★ Menstrual Moon Magick ★

Purpose

Perform this ritual monthly to ease and aid your menstrual cycle. This spell helps you to reconnect with the Lunar Goddess and retune your body to its natural rhythm. It can help to ease cramps, mood swings, and other period-related symptoms such as acne and bloating, as well as settling your cycle. Remember, when you're in tune with Mother Nature, your magick is always much stronger. If you're going through the menopause or suffering with PCOS (polycystic ovary syndrome), then this ritual is also a good one to use.

Lunar Phase

Perform this ritual on the first day of your menstrual cycle, or if you're not having periods or they're irregular, perform this monthly at the New Moon. If you're going through the menopause, perform this ritual during a Waning Moon.

Ingredients

~ Silver spell candle

~ Coconut essential oil*

~ Jasmine incense*

~ Moonstone tumblestone

~ Silver spell bag

* Optional but powerful

Method

1. Set your altar and cast your magick circle.

2. Carefully inscribe a simple U-shape on the silver spell candle to symbolize your womb.

3. If using coconut oil, anoint the candle working from wick to end until it's coated with a light layer.

4. Set the candle securely back in its holder and light it, along with your jasmine incense (if using).

5. Hold your moonstone in your left hand and say the verse:

> *Moonlight Goddess shining bright,*
> *Fill me with your healing light.*
> *As I am woman, we are one,*
> *Our gentle cycles ease us on.*

As we wane and as we wax,
My mind and body can relax.
As we wax and as we wane,
Ease all symptoms, strife, and pain.
As we're full and then are new,
My body flows at ease with you.

6. Place your moonstone next to the candle (allow it to burn down fully) and say:

I wish it, and so it is!

7. Close your magick circle and remember to ground yourself.

8. Once your spell is complete, place your moonstone in a silver spell bag and keep it with you, ideally in a trouser or skirt pocket, or attached to a belt – as close to your tummy as possible for seven days.

Action

As the spell candle burns down, practice some self-care. Surround yourself with soft blankets, cushions, and a hot-water bottle, and sip raspberry or chamomile tea as you practice simple breathing exercises, or listen to a chill-out playlist. Perform this ritual once a month, and use it as a reminder to book an appointment with your health practitioner for your regular smear test, mammogram, or female wellbeing check-up.

⋆★ Enchanted Moon Jewelry ★⋆

Purpose

This lovely little ritual can be used to charm a piece of jewelry such as a pendant, charm bracelet, or special ring. Once you've enchanted your jewelry with the magickal power of the Moon, wear it to protect and empower yourself when crafting wishes – or just to keep you connected to the magickal Moon every day. You can also give enchanted jewelry as a special gift, and let the receiver know that it's blessed with the magick of the Moon!

Lunar Phase

New, Waxing, or Full Moon

Ingredients

~   Silver spell candle

~   Jasmine incense

~   Special piece of jewelry (silver jewelry and jewelry made with moonstones or pearls works particularly well)

~   1 moonflower (or white rose)

~   Fennel seeds

~   Silver spell bag*

* Optional if giving as a gift

Method

1. Set your altar and cast your magick circle. If you can, set your altar outside on a summer's eve. If you can't work outside, a window ledge altar works too!

2. Light the silver spell candle and jasmine incense, and place the jewelry you wish to enchant in front of the candle, along with the flower.

3. Sprinkle three pinches of fennel seeds over the candle flame from a height and speak the spell:

> *Maiden quick and Maiden nimble,*
> *Mother fair, loving and humble,*
> *Crone of wisdom, sight, and power,*
> *Hear me in this Witching hour.*
> *Enchant and bless this sparkle charm*
> *With love and light and truth and calm.*
> *So when the wearer wishes cast,*
> *Come them true, and may they last.*
> *I ask tonight of Moon so sweet*
> *To make this magick sure and neat.*
> *By the power of three by three,*
> *Harm it none, and mote it be!*

4. Allow the candle to burn down fully and say:

> *I wish it, and so it is!*

5. Close your magick circle and remember to ground yourself.

6. Take the white flower and leave it outside as an offering of thanks to the Moon.

Action

Leave the jewelry on the window ledge until morning to charge fully with the Moon's power. If giving the jewelry as a gift, present it in a small silver satin or organza pouch, or a spell bag.

WISHES FOR CLEARING & CLEANSING

'Clarity within your vibrational energy embraces the
journey of your soul giving you clear direction.'

DEBBIE A. ANDERSON

Magickal Correspondences

Key word:	Clarify
Color:	White
Earth Treasure:	Clear quartz
Nature Gift:	White feather
Herb or spice:	Salt
Flower or plant:	Dandelion (seeding)
Incense:	White sage
Essential oil:	Sandalwood

⋆★ A Simple Cleansing Ritual ★⋆

Purpose

This simple ritual is great for clearing and cleansing anything - your home, your altar, your crystals, your magickal tools, and even yourself! Use it regularly to keep the energy around you cleansed, clear, and purified.

Lunar Phase

Any

Ingredients

~ White spell candle

~ White sage incense or smudge stick

~ Salt*

* Optional

Method

1. You don't need to set your altar, but do remember to cast your magick circle and light the white spell candle for the duration of this ritual. You can perform this ritual inside or outside.

2. Light the white sage incense or smudge stick and pass it carefully around the object or room you want to cleanse, making sure you go to the corners and behind the doors.

3. For each object or space you cleanse, simply say:

> *I cleanse and bless [this room/myself/this object] with love, light, and harmony.*
> *Blessed be!*

4. If you want to add extra power to your cleansing ritual, you can also sprinkle salt over or around the object or space you wish to clear. If you're cleansing yourself, you can sprinkle salt in a circle around yourself or even take a salt bath.

5. As you work, visualize a beautiful and clear white light filling you and surrounding you and the items and spaces you're working with.

6. When you're ready, blow out the candle and say:

> *I wish it, and so it is!*

7. Close your magick circle and remember to ground yourself.

8. Open as many doors and windows as you can for a few moments to allow any negative energy you've dispelled to be blown away - and invite in the fresh air to reinvigorate the atmosphere.

Action

Energy cleansing should be done alongside physical cleaning for the best results. If you're cleansing a room in your home, be sure to clear the physical clutter and dust before your ritual. If you're clearing yourself, take a beautiful bath first and maybe even take a detox day. Performing the ritual after this will leave you feeling purified and as fresh as a daisy, and will ensure that your magickal energy is performing at its optimum vibration.

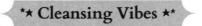

⋆ Cleansing Vibes ⋆

Purpose

As well as clearing our own auras, and the spaces and Cosmic energies that immediately surround us, we can all benefit from helping to clear the Universal energies across the world. Perform this ritual to send peaceful and loving vibes to an area of the world or to people who need them during unsettled times, and to bring more clarity and harmony into your own life, too.

Lunar Phase

Any

Ingredients

~ White spell candle

~ White sage incense

~ A fluffy dandelion (seeding)*

* Optional

Method

1. Set your altar and cast your magick circle. Carefully inscribe the words 'Peace,' 'Love,' and 'Harmony' into the white spell candle from wick to end.

2. Light the candle and the white sage incense and say:

> *By the power of three by three,*
> *Bring peace and love and harmony*
> *To all who need it, and to me.*
> *Harm it none, and mote it be!*

3. Allow the candle to burn down fully, and open a window to allow the peaceful vibes to be carried away to where they're most needed.

4. If you have a seeding dandelion, take it outside and puff away all the seeds. As you watch them float away on the breeze, know that the Universe has heard you and your positive energies are helping those who need healing, and say:

Should they wish it, so it is!

5. Close your magick circle and remember to ground yourself.

Action

If there's a need in the world such as a natural disaster, you can see what fundraising opportunities you can help with. Be a role model for harmony, peace, and love, and reach out to a friend or family member to see if they need help with anything. Be kind to yourself and practice meditation or relaxation. Make a commitment to live your life in balance and attuned to a higher vibration. Practice this ritual regularly to reconnect with your energy and the other positive energy sources that surround you.

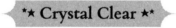

⋆⋆ Crystal Clear ⋆⋆

Purpose

This spell is really useful when you need help figuring out an answer to a problem or question, or just a little mental clearing and clarity. Perform this at any time, but a Full Moon sheds extra light on your challenges.

Lunar Phase

Any

Ingredients

~ White spell candle

~ White sage incense

~ Clear quartz tumblestone

Method

1. Set your altar and cast your magick circle.

2. Inscribe the white spell candle with the word 'Clarity' from wick to end, and on the opposite side, 'Confusion' from end to wick.

3. Light the candle and the white sage incense, and pass your clear quartz around them three times widdershins chanting 'Confusion,' and then three times deosil chanting 'Clarity.'

4. Take your clear quartz in your left hand and say:

Crystal bring me clarity,
Dispel all my uncertainty.
Bring the answers that I need,
My intuition I will heed.
Help me see the clearest way
As Earth turns from this night to day.

By the power of three by three,
With harm to none, so mote it be!

5. Meditate for a while on the candle flame, but for this spell try not to think about your question. Instead, practice a little mindfulness or simply relax, and when you feel your mind start to wander, bring your attention back to the flame and the feel of your clear quartz in your left hand.

6. Clear and release your mind of stress and anxiety to allow the magick to do its work.

7. When you feel ready, blow out the candle and say:

I wish it, and so it is!

8. Close your magick circle and remember to ground yourself.

Action

Place your clear quartz under your pillow. Take some time out before you sleep to do something you enjoy and that you find relaxing: read, write in your gratitude journal, or watch your favorite guilty pleasure TV show with a warm bedtime drink. Trust that the answers will come to you in the morning!

WISHES FOR POWER & PROTECTION

'Real magic is not about gaining power over others: it is about gaining power over yourself.'

ROSEMARY ELLEN GUILEY

Magickal Correspondences

Key words:	Psychic power
Color:	Purple
Earth Treasure:	Amethyst
Nature Gift:	Acorn
Herb or spice:	Cloves
Flower or plant:	Angelica
Incense:	Dragon's blood resin
Essential oil:	Amber

⋆★ A Personal Power Ritual ★⋆

Purpose

This spell is all about psychic protection and developing your own personal pool of power. Perform this ritual when you have plenty of time preferably: I would suggest giving yourself at least 45 minutes to an hour if you can. The longer you can meditate with this ritual, the more you'll be able to focus and work with your own energies.

Purple signifies power, protection, and psychic awareness, and white symbolizes truth and purity. This spell brings both together to ask the Universe to help you work powerful magick with positivity, clarity, and good intentions. And don't be put off by the dragon's blood resin incense this spell calls for - it's just made from the dark red sap of a tree and is widely available online and in MBS stores.

Lunar Phase

New, Waxing, or Full Moon

Ingredients

~ 2 x 1 ft (30cm) lengths of ribbon or thread (1 purple and 1 white)

~ Purple spell candle

~ White spell candle

~ Sticky tack

~ Dragon's blood resin incense*

~ Photograph of yourself

~ Amethyst tumblestone

~ Clear quartz tumblestone

* Optional

Method

1. Set your altar and cast your magick circle.

2. Spend some time entwining the purple and white ribbons around your two spell candles, binding them together. Just make sure to tie your ribbons a good 2-3in (5-7.5cm) away from the candle wicks.

3. As you work, think about your magickal journey so far and what you'd like to achieve and learn as a new or developing witch.

4. Place the twined candles on a candle plate - you can use sticky tack to hold them upright and securely in place - and light them both. Light the dragon's blood resin incense (if using).

5. Next, take your photograph and position your amethyst on the center of your forehead in the image, and your

clear quartz above your head (it doesn't matter if this means the crystal is above the photograph). This aligns your third eye and crown chakras responsible for psychic awareness and higher consciousness.

6. Spend a moment sending love, light, and protection to yourself in your photograph, and when you're ready, say the following verse:

> *Universe, I ask of you,*
> *That spells I work be pure and true.*
> *'Tis the day my wings take flight,*
> *A magick soul of love and light.*
> *As comes the day, so comes the night.*
>
> *Within my heart, my power dwells,*
> *And when I work my WishCraft spells,*
> *Abundance, joy, and love will bring,*
> *When this goodly witch doth sing.*
>
> *As above and so below,*
> *When this life ebbs to and fro,*
> *In my strength I know and trust,*
> *The power mine to use is just.*
>
> *As within and as without,*
> *When the circle turns about,*
> *Earth and Fire, Water, Air,*
> *Spirits, harken to my prayer.*

As I am blessed, so I be charmed,
Protected, safe, and never harmed.
And harm no other, three by three,
What's wished is done
And blessed be!

7. Focus on the candle flames and clear your mind.

8. Relax and enjoy this special moment to connect with the Universe, and mentally note what thoughts and feelings come to you – but try, if you can, not to hold on to them.

9. Allow yourself to release any self-doubt, and notice the positive energy both around and within you.

10. Make sure to extinguish the candles before the flames reach the ribbons, close your magick circle, and remember to ground yourself.

Action

If any thoughts and feelings stay with you after the ritual, be sure to make a note of them in your WishCraft journal and see what comes up for you – perhaps they're things you need to explore further or work on. Practice this ritual whenever you want to deepen your connection with your personal power and Spirit. Keep your photograph in your journal or your wallet as a reminder of your special connection to the Universe.

⋆★ Crystals of Protection ★⋆

Purpose

Mirrors or reflective surfaces have long been considered to reflect negativity and ward off evil intentions. We use a mirror in this spell to deflect negative vibes. This charm will protect you from astral attacks and psychic vampires – those who feed off our emotions and drain us mentally and physically. You'll also be protected from other people's negativity.

Lunar Phase

Waxing or Full Moon

Ingredients

~ Purple spell candle

~ 3 cloves

~ Dragon's blood resin incense

~ Amethyst tumblestone

~ Small mirror

~ Purple spell bag

Method

1. Set your altar and cast your magick circle.

2. Inscribe the purple spell candle for 'Protection' from wick to end, then carefully push the three cloves into the candle in a vertical line from wick to end.

3. Light the candle and the dragon's blood resin incense, and take your amethyst in your left hand. Hold the mirror in your right hand – turned away from you, facing outward – and say:

> *Safe, protected, and free from harm,*
> *This crystal be my lucky charm.*
> *Deflecting ill away from me,*
> *Warmth and love are all I see.*
> *As this mirror me defends,*
> *Prayers I send to spirit friends*
> *And ask of them to keep me free*
> *From others' negativity.*
> *And by the power of three by three,*
> *With harm to none so mote it be!*

4. Spend a few moments visualizing a bright purple light emanating from your amethyst and completely enveloping you.

5. Feel the positivity, power, and safety of the energetic vibrations surrounding you and know that you're fully protected and safe.

6. When you're ready, blow out the candle and say:

I wish it, and so it is!

7. Place your amethyst in the spell bag and keep it with you as your talisman of protection.

8. Close your magick circle and remember to ground yourself.

9. Repeat this enchantment once a month to keep your protection energy strong and ward off any negative vibes.

Action

Whenever you look in the mirror – to brush your hair or brush your teeth – smile at yourself and affirm:

I am protected, and I am safe.

You'll be surprised how this regular affirmation will aid your general sense of confidence and wellbeing.

Try a little game next time you're outside: take your protection amethyst with you and keep it in your pocket or purse. As you walk along, imagine your bright purple circle of protection surrounding you and visualize it like a solid wall of light that goes with you wherever you walk. Watch how people move and disperse around it, unconsciously aware of your protected personal space. It's pretty cool, and kind of fun (and especially useful in crowded places!).

★ Increase your Psychic Awareness ★

Purpose

This ritual will help to open your channels of psychic perception. Practice it to develop your psychic abilities and strengthen your Cosmic connections. Include your personal protection crystal to keep your energy positive throughout. This spell calls for relaxation and visualization rather than spoken words. The more you do this the easier it will become.

Lunar Phase

Any

Ingredients

~ Relaxing sounds playlist

~ Small mirror

~ Goddess candle

~ Purple spell candle

~ Dragon's blood resin incense

~ Amethyst protection crystal

~ Your WishCraft journal and a pen

Method

1. Set your altar and cast your magick circle, then dim the lights and set your relaxation playlist to an ambient volume.

2. Place the mirror between your Goddess and purple spell candles, facing upward so that the mirror can deflect all but positive and happy energy away from your circle.

3. Light the purple spell candle and incense, and spend a few moments breathing deeply and allowing yourself to focus on the candle flame.

4. Next, take your amethyst protection crystal in your left hand and place it in the center of your forehead: the location of your third eye chakra.

5. As you do this, imagine your third eye like a beautiful purple flower unfurling and opening its petals, allowing you to connect the seen with the unseen, and the known with the unknown.

6. Place your amethyst protection crystal back on your altar and rest your hands in your lap. Breathe easily and focus on the candle flame.

7. As you relax, you'll start to notice images appearing in your mind's eye. Some may be scenes of the past or present; as you become more adept, you'll begin to see flashes from the future too.

8. Try not to 'hold on' to these images; simply notice them and allow them to come and go. Are there any patterns to the images? Are there any themes? Is there anything that strikes you as particularly important – something you need to pay attention to or something you need to learn from?

9. Don't worry if you don't notice any patterns or significance to the images at first, just allow the pictures in your mind to come and go.

10. When you feel ready, extinguish the candle and take a moment to reconnect with the world around you as everything comes gently back into focus.

11. Thank any spirits or deities you have called upon for protection and assistance. Close your magick circle and remember to ground yourself.

Action

Make a note in your journal of any images, thoughts, or feelings that have stayed with you or stand out to you. Practice this ritual regularly and keep a record of your visions – this will help you to link them together and make sense of what you've seen, offering insights and lessons for the past, the present, and the future and strengthening the power of your magickal work.

WISHES FOR MIDNIGHT MAGICK

'Every great dream begins with a dreamer.'

HARRIET TUBMAN

Magickal Correspondences

Key word:	Wisdom
Color:	Dark blue
Earth Treasure:	Sodalite
Nature Gift:	Owl feathers
Herb or spice:	Lavender
Flower or plant:	Enchanter's nightshade
Incense:	Opium
Essential oil:	Valerian

⋆★ A Wish to Recall Your Dreams ★⋆

Purpose

This spell helps to recall your dreams so that you can note them and begin to unveil the secrets of your subconscious. Sodalite is a crystal long associated with communication and understanding. This spell also calls on the wisdom of the nocturnal owl to aid you in deciphering the messages received when you sleep.

Lunar Phase

Any

Ingredients

- ~ Dark blue spell candle

- ~ Opium incense

- ~ Sodalite tumblestone

- ~ Dark blue spell bag

- ~ Owl feather, ornament, or picture

Method

1. Set your altar and cast your magick circle.

2. Inscribe the dark blue spell candle wick to end with the words: 'Wisdom,' 'Dreams,' 'Recall,' and 'Remember.'

3. Secure the candle in its holder and light it, then light the opium incense from the flame.

4. Focus on the candle, and allow your mind to clear and your body to relax as much as you can.

5. Pass your sodalite around the candle flame three times deosil, and repeat this verse three times:

> *Midnight dreams that come to me,*
> *Bring wisdom, sight, and clarity.*
> *In the morn I shall recall*
> *To understand once and for all!*
> *By the power of three by three,*
> *Harm it none, and mote it be!*

6. Hold your sodalite in your left hand and meditate for a few moments on the candle flame.

7. Visualize a beautiful, bright owl bringing messages to you as you sleep. Make this image as big and clear and bright in your mind as you can.

8. When you feel ready, blow out your candle and say:

> *I wish it, and so it is!*

9. Close your magick circle and remember to ground yourself.

Action

Place your sodalite in the blue spell bag and keep it under your pillow. Each night before you go to sleep, meditate with it for a few moments by taking it out and holding it in your left hand. Place your owl feather, ornament, or picture on your bedside table or dresser where you'll see it first thing in the morning – the spirit of your spell owl will remind you to remember your dream and write it down in your journal straight away, bringing you useful insight and wisdom.

★ A Ritual for Restful Sleep ★

Purpose

Perform this ritual any time you need to get a good night's sleep. Drift off gently, and awaken feeling rested and refreshed.

Lunar Phase

Any

Ingredients

~ Dark blue spell candle

~ Cup of chamomile tea

~ Lavender incense

~ 9 pinches of lavender (fresh or dried)

~ Dark blue spell bag

Method

1. You don't need to set your altar for this ritual, but you can cast your magick circle if you wish.

2. Prepare your space for sleep by opening the window to cool down your room, dimming the lights, and ensuring you're as relaxed and comfortable as you can be.

3. Set up the dark blue spell candle safely away from any soft furnishings and make sure you extinguish it fully before getting into bed.

4. As you sip your chamomile tea, spend a moment inscribing the words 'Sleep,' 'Relax,' and 'Rest' on the candle from wick to end.

5. Light the candle and the incense, and spend a few minutes making a little sleep pouch with the lavender and the spell bag.

6. When you're ready, say the verse:

> Now the day has turned to night,
> Lay me down and sleep me tight.
> Awake tomorrow, fresh and new,
> To the scent of morning dew.

7. Extinguish the candle, finish your tea, and place your lavender sleep spell pouch under your pillow or hang it on your headboard and say:

I wish it, and so it is!

8. Close your magick circle and remember to ground yourself.

Action

If, like me, you're prone to insomnia, try and make this ritual part of your evening routine on a regular basis. You could even extend the ritual to allow a little more time to wind down and relax by spending 10 minutes writing in your journal, reading a sleepy poem, or even coloring a picture.

⋆ Secret Starlight Wishes ⋆

Purpose

This cute, all-purpose wishing charm is simple but powerful. It's best worked under a night sky when the stars are bright. The most important element of this ritual is to really think about your wish and how you phrase it – remember the WishCraft rules: your wish should be positive, specific, and actionable. If you happen to see a shooting star as you craft your wish, it's a sure sign from the Universe that your request has been heard and good things are soon to come your way!

Lunar Phase

New or Waxing Moon

Ingredients

~   Dark blue spell candle

~   Spell candle in a complementary color for your wish

~   Yellow, gold, or silver craft card

~   Ruler, pencil, and craft scissors

~   Felt-tip pen in a complementary color for your wish

~   Craft glue*

~   Gold or silver glitter*

~   Thin gold or silver ribbon

~   3 pinches of lavender (fresh or dried)

* Optional but pretty!

Method

1. Set your altar and cast your magick circle.

2. Inscribe the dark blue spell candle with the phrase: 'I wish it, and so it is!' and the colored spell candle with a single word summing up your wish (for example, 'Home,' 'Love,' or 'Health') from wick to end.

3. Light both candles and set to work on the star!

4. Using a ruler if you like, draw a five-point star on the craft card and carefully cut it out. The size is up to you, but make sure it's big enough to write your wish on and to decorate if you want to.

5. On one side of the star, write out your wish with the felt-tip pen. Be specific – for example, 'I wish for a new home by the beach, with three bedrooms and a big garden for the dog that I can easily afford.'

6. You can decorate the other side of the star with pictures that represent all the elements of your wish – if you're wishing for love you might draw hearts, or if you're wishing for a new home, perhaps you'll draw a key. To win a race or a sporting competition, you could draw a medal or a rosette. If you like, you can add some glue and glitter and make it super sparkly and pretty (who doesn't love a few sparkles?!).

7. Finally, using a pencil, carefully make a small hole in the top arm of the star (make sure it's the right way up) and thread through your ribbon and tie it to make a loop.

8. Once it's done and dry, take the star in both hands, focus on the candles and say:

> Twinkle, twinkle shining stars,
> Lighting up the night.
> This little wish I send to you,
> To make it true and bright.

I wish, I wish upon a star
My hopes and dreams come true.
As I know now what you are,
And the Magick that you do.
With harm to none and three by three,
I trust my wish to you!

9. Sprinkle a pinch of lavender from a height over the candle flame and whisper:

    I wish it, and so it is!

10. Extinguish the candle and open a window to allow your magick to be set free.

11. Close your magick circle and remember to ground yourself.

12. Hang the star somewhere you'll see it every day!

Action

Whatever you wish, take action within 24 hours to show the Universe that you're ready and willing to work for your wish! If you wished for good health, join a gym or start a fitness class. If you wished for a new home, contact an estate agent or realtor – even if you don't think you're able to move just yet, remember that magick can happen in the most mysterious of ways. Show the Universe you're ready and waiting, and serious about getting your wish!

WISHES FOR HEALTH & WELLBEING

'We all have the ability to heal ourselves; I know,
I have done so… know that you are Loved.'

LISA BELLINI

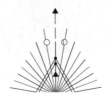

Magickal Correspondences

Key word:	Healing
Color:	Light blue
Earth Treasure:	Blue lace agate
Nature Gift:	Seashells
Herb or spice:	Basil
Flower or plant:	Aloe vera
Incense:	Eucalyptus
Essential oil:	Chamomile

⋆ Healing Wishes ⋆

Purpose

This gentle all-purpose healing ritual can be adapted for most minor illnesses and ailments in humans and animals. It can also help with a wildlife sickness outbreak. Remember that all spells cast on others, including healing spells, should have the recipient's permission – so ask them first. If you're casting for an animal or for wildlife, change the phrase 'I wish it, and so it is!' to 'Should they wish it, so it is!' Your furry or feathery recipients will then have the choice whether or not to accept the magick you've sent their way.

Lunar Phase

Any (but New or Waxing Moons are best)

Ingredients

- ~ Light blue spell candle
- ~ Eucalyptus essential oil*
- ~ Photo, memento, or some representation of the person or animal/s you wish to heal
- ~ Blue lace agate tumblestone
- ~ 12 pinches of basil (finely chopped, fresh or dried)
- ~ Light blue spell bag

* Optional

Method

1. Set your altar and cast your magick circle.

2. Inscribe the light-blue candle with the name of the person or animal you wish to heal (or your own name if the spell is for yourself!). If you're using the eucalyptus essential oil, anoint the candle from wick to end.

3. Place the photo or other item in front of the candle with your blue lace agate on top.

4. Light the candle and chant the verse:

> *Candle, candle burning bright,*
> *Bless me [or insert name] with your healing light.*
> *Help to mend [my/his/her/their] ills and ails,*
> *That wholeness, health, and strength prevails.*
> *By the power of three by three,*
> *Harm done to none and mote it be!*

5. Take your blue lace agate and pass it three times deosil around the candle.

6. Sprinkle three pinches of basil from a height over the candle flame and say:

> *I wish it, and so it is!*

7. Allow the candle to burn down fully and add nine pinches of basil and your blue lace agate to the spell bag.

8. Close your magick circle and remember to ground yourself.

Action

If the spell is for a friend or family member, give them the charm – and maybe a bunch of grapes, too! If the charm is for a pet or small child, keep it close to where they sleep (but out of harm's way). If the charm is for nature or wildlife, hang it on a tree, bury the stone and herbs in the earth, or give them to a river or ocean (without the spell bag). If you're healing yourself, keep the charm with you for seven days and do whatever you can to take care of yourself until you're feeling better!

★ A Wellbeing Wish ★

Purpose

Drawing on the healing and calming properties of Water, this peaceful enchantment will bring a sense of harmony and balance when you need to realign. Take time out to enjoy performing this ritual. If you live near the ocean, a river, or a stream, this is a lovely spell to do outside on a pleasant day. If you're in the city, or the weather is bad, pop on your water sounds playlist and invite the Water Elementals (Undines) inside.

Lunar Phase

Any

Ingredients

~ Light-blue spell candle

~ Chamomile incense

~ Water (if at home, a bowl of spring water from a bottle works fine)

~ Your favorite water sounds playlist*

~ Blue lace agate tumblestone

* Optional

Method

1. You don't need to set a full altar for this ritual, but remember to cast your magick circle.

2. Inscribe the light-blue spell candle with the word 'Tranquility' from wick to end, and light it, along with the chamomile incense, near a natural source of water or on a window ledge next to a bowl of spring water. If you're indoors, you can set your relaxing water sounds playlist to an ambient volume and recite the words:

> *Ocean waves and babbling brooks,*
> *Waterfalls and winding rivers,*
> *Gentle rain and curling streams,*

Puddles, lakes, and ripples,
Wash away the stress and strains
And bring your calm vibrations.
Relaxed and eased of body and mind
And cleansed of all distractions.

3. With your blue lace agate in your left hand, sit comfortably and gaze into the water.

4. Enjoy the soothing sounds and allow your mind to clear and release any tension. Breathe easily, feel your muscles soften, and visualize all your troubles being washed away by the water, leaving you perfectly calm, relaxed, and at ease.

5. Allow the candle to burn down completely, cleanse your blue lace agate in the bowl of water, or in an ocean or stream, and thank the Undines for their calming and cleansing vibrations.

6. Close your magick circle and remember to ground yourself.

Action

Meditation, mindfulness, and relaxation are vitally important to our mental and physical wellbeing. Practice this calming water ritual as often as you need to stay in tune with the natural tides of your own mind and body, and as part of a blissful wellbeing and self-care routine.

⋆⋆ Angel Wishes Healing Spell ⋆⋆

Purpose

Use this spell to heal a specific illness or ailment. You can adapt the wording of the spell to focus on a specific person, animal, or area of the body. This spell calls on the angel of healing, Raphael, and is particularly useful when facing a stay in hospital or an operation to aid a speedy and safe recovery.

Lunar Phase

New or Waxing Moon

Ingredients

~ Picture or representation of an angel (an ornament, an angel wing charm, or a white feather)

~ Light-blue spell candle

~ Chamomile essential oil

~ 9 pinches of basil (finely chopped, fresh or dried)

~ Piece of paper

~ Eucalyptus incense

~ Blue lace agate tumblestone

~ Blue spell bag

Method

1. Set your altar, including your angel picture or representation, and cast your magick circle.

2. Inscribe the light-blue spell candle from wick to end with the words 'Healing,' 'Health,' and 'Recovery,' and the name of the person or animal you're healing; and from end to wick with the word 'Illness' or the name of the ailment – for example, 'Infection' or 'Broken bone.'

3. Anoint the candle with the chamomile essential oil and scatter the basil over the paper.

4. Roll the candle across the paper so that the herbs stick to the oil and give the candle a light coating.

5. Light the candle and the eucalyptus incense, and, holding your blue lace agate in your left hand, close your eyes and ask the Angel Raphael to join you in your magick circle.

6. Meditate on the candle flame and say:

   [The name of the person or animal you wish to heal],
   I cast this spell for your healing, only with your
   blessing and with true and good intent.

7. Add your blue lace agate to the spell bag along with the leftover basil. Tie it securely and hold it in your left hand close to your heart as you cast the spell:

I call the spirits from above,
With thoughts of healing and of love,
That they may bless this magick charm
With health and healing and no harm,
And that they stay with you until
You are well and no more ill.

I ask the Angel on this night,
To keep you safe and hold you tight.
This spell directs your [bone/heart/lungs, etc.] to heal,
I know this magick to be real,
And when you wake the work be done
Soon again you'll walk and run.
Back at home you soon will be,
Recovered, well, safe, and free.
So by the power of three by three
With harm to none so mote it be!

8. Take the spell bag and pass it around the candle flame three times widdershins, chanting 'Ailment' as you do so; and then pass the spell bag three times deosil around the candle flame, chanting 'Recovery.'

9. Extinguish the candle and say:

   I wish it, and so it is! [Or *Should they wish it, so it is!*]

10. Thank Raphael and the angels for hearing your prayer.

11. Close your magick circle and remember to ground yourself.

Action

If you can, give the charm to the person you were casting the spell for to keep by their bedside. If the charm is for a pet or a small child, keep it close to where they sleep but out of harm's way. If the charm is for a wild animal, you can tie it to a tree branch or hang it in your garden – anywhere outside. Ensure you also follow through (or help the patient follow through) with any prescribed treatments and medications, and supplement your treatment regimen with a healthy diet and any other homeopathic and complementary therapies that are recommended.

WISHES FOR MONEY & LUCK

'All that is mine by Divine Right is now released and reaches me in great avalanches of abundance.'

FLORENCE SCOVEL SHINN

Magickal Correspondences

Key word:	Abundance
Color:	Green
Earth Treasure:	Green jade
Nature Gift:	Conker (buckeye)
Herb or spice:	Mint
Flower or plant:	Honeysuckle
Incense:	Frankincense
Essential oil:	Bergamot

⋆ Wishing Well Spell ⋆

Purpose

If you've been feeling a financial pinch, then the Wishing Well Spell is the perfect way to manifest more money! If your well (or your bank balance) is running dry, use this ritual to ask the Universe to send more money your way and keep your flow of income abundant.

Lunar Phase

Waxing Moon

Ingredients

~   Green spell candle

~   Penny or cent coin

~   3 pinches of mint (finely chopped, fresh or dried)

~   Jade tumblestone

Method

1. Set your altar and cast your magick circle.

2. Inscribe the green spell candle wick to end with words and symbols that represent actual money to you (for example, 'Cash,' '£££,' or '$$$'), and the specific amount of money you would like to receive.

3. Light the candle and carefully drip three drops of wax on to the coin, saying the amount you need out loud three times as you do so, and then replace the candle in the holder.

4. Sprinkle three pinches of mint onto the wax, and allow it to cool as you cast your wish:

> *Magick Penny, bring to me*
> *The [insert amount] that I need!*
> *You are my blessed Wishing Well,*
> *So multiply and heed my spell.*
> *By the power of three by three,*
> *With harm to none, so mote it be!*

5. Once you're sure the wax on the coin is dry, hold it in your left hand along with your jade.

6. Meditate on the candle flame and daydream about opening your purse or your bank statement and seeing the exact amount you've asked for. Make the image as bright and clear as you can in your mind – imagine the texture of the notes in your hands, and how it would feel to have all the money you needed. Ask the Universe to help you make it happen!

7. When you feel ready, blow out the candle and say:

> *I wish it, and so it is!*

8. Close your magick circle and remember to ground yourself.

9. Pop the penny or cent in your purse or wallet and trust that the money you need is coming to you.

Action

Sometimes sources of income can spring up in surprising ways! Maybe you'll discover an old treasure in the attic you could sell online? Have you got any old investment accounts that kind relatives set up for you when you were young that you've forgotten about? What about a skill or talent that you've always thought about making into a business? Now would be a great time to get started!

★ A Magick Money Tree ★

Purpose

When my daughters were younger, I'd often find myself telling them when they asked for things that 'Money doesn't grow on trees' and that I couldn't 'Magick money out of thin air.' As it transpires, you can absolutely magick money out of thin air. This spell is a little more complex, but well worth it.

This ritual calls for a physical tree (or plant). Honeysuckle is the traditional plant witches use to attract money and abundance, but if you can't use honeysuckle you can use another plant or tree – apple trees, oak trees, maple trees, and even bonsai trees are associated with luck, money, and abundance – so use whatever you have or can find that feels right for you. The more of the ingredients you can include in this spell, the more powerful your money-attracting energy will be – throw everything you can at this one, and the Universe will throw money right back at you from literally all directions!

Lunar Phase

New, Waxing, or Full Moon

Ingredients

~ Potted honeysuckle (or any suitable tree)

~ Green spell candle

~ Bergamot essential oil

~ Frankincense incense

~ Small dish of mint (finely chopped, fresh or dried)

~ 9 lengths of thin green ribbon, each roughly 9in (23cm) long

~ Conker (buckeye), or jade tumblestone

Method

1. If your tree or plant is already outside, work this enchantment on a fine day and set your altar on a small patio table or on the ground.

2. Cast your magick circle around your altar and your tree or plant of choice.

3. Inscribe the green spell candle with the words 'Magick Me Money' from wick to end, and then anoint it with bergamot oil.

4. Light the candle along with the frankincense incense.

5. Next, take the dish of mint and work deosil, sprinkling a circle around your tree or plant.

6. Then, take the nine green ribbons and tie them in bows on various branches of your plant or tree - take care not to break any delicate stems or damage it in any way.

7. Sprinkle three pinches of mint on the candle flame and say:

Magick, magick money tree,
Blessed with luck and money be!
Send gifts of cash, dear Universe,
To fill my bank and fill my purse.
May I be rich and blessed and wealthy,
And those I love kept safe and healthy.
By the power of three by three,
With harm to none, so mote it be!

8. Finally, bury the conker or jade in the pot with your plant, or at the base of your tree as an offering of thanks.

9. Allow the candle to burn down completely and say:

I wish it, and so it is!

10. Close your magick circle and remember to ground yourself.

11. Water your tree or plant in hot weather and tend to it, and the Universe will attend to your financial needs in return.

Action

Remember that the Universe can help us most when we help ourselves. Take some time to think about what has been holding you back from having enough money in the past – is it a lack of confidence to go for that job or promotion you'd like? Perhaps it's negative fears or feelings about money that stem from your past, or a lack of belief in your deserving of wealth? Now would be an awesome time to find yourself a life coach or a money coach, or see a financial advisor and take control of any savings or investments you have or perhaps open a savings account. And remember that from little acorns, mighty oaks do grow!

★ Bee Lucky ★

Purpose

Perform this every time you need a boost of extra luck, to dispel a streak of bad luck, or just to manifest more good luck in your life. For me, bees are incredibly lucky. Whenever I see bees, I magickally receive abundance or good fortune! Through the ages, bees have provided sustenance with their sweet honey and even wax for our candles, so I created this spell to honor our little busy buddies.

Lunar Phase

Waxing Moon

Ingredients

~ Green spell candle

~ Teaspoon of clear honey

~ 3 pinches of mint (finely chopped, fresh or dried)

~ Jade tumblestone

Method

1. Set your altar and cast your magick circle.

2. Inscribe the green spell candle with the words 'Good luck,' 'Prosperity,' and 'Abundance' from wick to end.

3. Anoint the candle with a thin layer of the sticky honey, working from wick to end all the way around until it's completely coated.

4. Sprinkle a piece of paper with the mint and roll the candle across the page so that the mint sticks to the honey.

5. Replace the candle in its holder, light it, and recite the incantation three times:

> *Just like honey to a bee,*
> *Good luck sticks itself to me!*
> *By the power of three by three,*
> *With harm to none, so mote it be.*

6. Take your jade and hold it in your left hand. Spend a few minutes visualizing and practicing what it feels like to suddenly become the luckiest person in the world. Let your mind know no limits – because your magick knows no limits!

7. Take a moment to journal about all the extravagant, amazing, and wonderful opportunities you're about to experience.

8. When you feel ready, pass your jade around the candle three times deosil, chanting:

> *Be lucky, be lucky, be lucky!*

9. Blow out the candle and say:

I wish it, and so it is!

10. Close your magick circle and remember to ground yourself.

Action

Take a positive action within 24 hours to set your magick in motion! Enter a (free) competition or prize draw, send off your CV for a new job, apply for something, or organize a fun night out with the girls at the bingo – it might just be your lucky day!

WISHES FOR SUCCESS & ACHIEVEMENT

'I learned early on the magic of life is having a
vision, having faith, and then going for it.'

ELAINE WELTEROTH

Magickal Correspondences

Key word:	Achievement
Color:	Yellow
Earth Treasure:	Citrine
Nature Gift:	Pinecones
Herb or spice:	Allspice
Flower or plant:	Marigold
Incense:	Bayberry
Essential oil:	Lemon

⋆⋆ Seeds of Success! ⋆⋆

Purpose

This spell is one for the long game! Sowing the seeds of your plans and nurturing them to fruition can take many months but, like your dreams and goals, the beautiful blooms are well worth working (and waiting) for! Taking care of your plant ensures you maintain your focus, and as your flowers blossom, so will your success. You can use any yellow flowering seeds or plant for your project, but one that works particularly well is coronilla. Once established, coronilla brings cheerful yellow pea-like blooms to your garden during the colder months and is easy to care for, tough, hardy, and resilient. Sometimes you also need to embody a tenacious determination to fulfill your destiny, and coronilla in full bloom is reminiscent of the success that crowns your wishes. Time your spell according to the planting instructions of your seeds or young plant in the spring.

Lunar Phase

New Moon

Ingredients

~   Coronilla seeds or pot plant (or marigolds)

~   Yellow spell candle

~ Yellow pencil or felt-tip pen

~ Your WishCraft journal

~ Large outdoor planting container or suitable garden spot and planting soil

Method

1. Set your altar with the seeds, bulbs, or pot plant upon it and cast your magick circle.

2. Light the yellow spell candle and spend some time writing down your goal or dream in your journal. Is it starting your own business? Learning to drive? Buying your first home or moving abroad?

3. Use positive words as you write very clearly what it is you want, and then spend some time thinking about what steps you need to take to achieve it, such as speaking to a career advisor or a recruitment agent, or starting a course.

4. Get down to the nitty-gritty of your goal and work out a monthly savings target or a list of websites you can use to research and make an action plan.

5. When you're ready, place your left hand on your seeds or plant and say:

> *Little yellow flower,*
> *Success is in your power.*
> *As you grow and flourish,*

My plans and dreams you nourish.
When your blooms I see,
My goal will come to be.
By the power of three by three,
With harm to none and mote it be!

6. Allow the candle to burn out and say:

I wish it, and so it is!

7. Plant your seeds or position your pot as instructed and close your magick circle, remembering to ground yourself afterward.

Action

Be sure to take good care of your plant or seeds until they're well established. Apply this care and attention to your goals and dreams, make a start on your action plan, and expect the results you seek in 6–12 months (or when your flowers bloom).

⋆ A Wish to Pass a Test ⋆

Purpose

This all-purpose test-passing luck charm can help you keep your nerves under control and bring you magickal focus, clarity, and a sense of calm on the big day. Adapt it to use for anything from an important exam to a driving test.

Lunar Phase
New Moon

Ingredients
~ Yellow spell candle

~ Bayberry incense*

~ Citrine tumblestone

~ Yellow spell bag

~ 3 pinches of allspice

~ Lucky clover (ideally a real one, or you can use a picture)*

* Optional but very helpful!

Method
1. Set your altar and cast your magick circle.

2. Inscribe the name of the test or exam you wish to pass on the yellow spell candle from wick to end, and light it along with the bayberry incense (if using).

3. Hold your citrine in your left hand and repeat the incantation nine times:

I will do well.
Be at my best.
I cast my spell
To pass this test.

4. Focus on the candle flame and visualize passing your test or exam. Imagine feeling calm, assured, and completely confident. Visualize and feel the empowerment of knowing everything you need to know, and doing everything you need to do with assurance, ease, and clarity. Allow yourself to feel the feelings of having full trust in your skills and abilities. Imagine receiving your result and visualize your pass mark. Make the image as clear and big and bright as you can in your mind's eye, and feel all the pleasure, joy, and achievement of having already achieved the result you desire... it's already done!

5. Pop your citrine in your spell bag and add three pinches of allspice and the clover.

6. Enchant your lucky charm by passing it three times deosil around the candle flame, chanting:

I will pass my test.

7. Extinguish the candle and say:

I wish it, and so it is!

8. Close your magick circle and remember to ground yourself. Be sure to keep your lucky test-passing charm with you on the day!

Action

Do all the preparation you possibly can for your exam or test, and know that the Universe will come to your aid on the day and ensure everything goes as smoothly and easily for you as possible. Take a deep breath and smash it out of the park! You got this!

★ Superpower Success Spray ★

Purpose

How cool would it be if you could 'bottle' success? Well, ta-da! Now you can. This super cool little enchantment does just that: perform this ritual to bottle success and create a nifty spray that you can spritz to bring the energy and vibration of success wherever you go... plus, it smells delicious, too! You can make your Superpower Success Spray with either fresh or dried petals, essential oils, or a mix of both (the fresh herbs look really pretty in the bottle and last longer than you'd expect due to the alcohol content). Use it when you're taking a test or exam, having an interview, or going for an important meeting – or whenever, just to remind yourself that you're a super successful and very awesome person!

Lunar Phase
Waxing Moon

Ingredients
~   Yellow spell candle

~   Bayberry incense*

~   Small pump spray bottle (a rinsed-out used bottle, or you can buy them cheaply)

~   3 fl.oz/90ml of distilled water

~   1 tbsp of alcohol (you can buy cleaning alcohol, or you can use vodka)

~   9 drops of lemon essential oil

~   3 pinches of allspice

~   13 yellow marigold petals

~   Small citrine tumblestone or crystal chip

~   Adhesive label and yellow felt-tip pen

~   Thin yellow ribbon

* Optional but super powerful

Method

1. Set your altar and cast your magick circle, placing all your spell ingredients within easy reach.

2. Inscribe the yellow spell candle with the word 'Success' from wick to end, and light it along with the bayberry incense (if using).

3. Add the water, alcohol, essential oil, spice, petals, and your citrine to the spray bottle, replace the lid securely and gently shake.

4. Pass the bottle around the candle flame three times deosil and say:

> *I charm this spray with great success.*
> *I will not settle for any less.*
> *In my dreams I will believe*
> *And know I can success achieve.*
> *With harm to none and three by three,*
> *Success is mine! So mote it be!*

5. Write 'Success Spray' on a sticky label in yellow pen and label your bottle, and if you like, tie a little yellow ribbon around the bottle neck in a cute bow.

6. Leave your bottle next to the candle, and allow the candle to burn down completely to fully charge your spray. Voila!

7. Say:

I wish it, and so it is!

8. Close your magick circle and remember to ground yourself.

Action

I love to spritz this when I'm driving in my car, and then blast out my favorite confidence-boosting playlist. It calms my nerves and reminds me that I can achieve anything. Armed with your Superpower Success Spray, you're set for anything and the world is your oyster – so go get 'em, girl!

WISHES FOR POSITIVITY & VITALITY

'If you change the way you look at things,
the things you look at change.'

DR. WAYNE W. DYER

Magickal Correspondences

Key word:	Optimism
Color:	Orange
Earth Treasure:	Carnelian tumblestone
Nature Gift:	Smooth pebbles
Herb or spice:	Ginger
Flower or plant:	Geranium
Incense:	Benzoin
Essential oil:	Cedar

✦ Positive Vibes ✦

Purpose

This lovely ritual brings a positive boost of joyful energy into your home or personal space whenever you're feeling a little down (and let's face it, sometimes we all do!). Use it to pep you up and bring your focus back to all that is healthy, happy, and vibrant.

Lunar Phase

Any

Ingredients

~ Orange spell candle

~ 3 drops of geranium essential oil

~ 3 pinches of ground ginger

~ Piece of paper

~ Benzoin incense*

~ Carnelian tumblestone

* Optional

Method

1. You don't need to set up your full altar for this spell, although of course you can if you wish - but this spell can easily be performed on a windowsill or mantelpiece in your home. Always remember to cast your magick circle.

2. Inscribe the orange spell candle with 'Positive vibes' from wick to end, and anoint it with the geranium essential oil.

3. Scatter the ginger on a piece of paper and roll the candle over the herbs to coat it lightly.

4. Light the candle and the benzoin incense, and place your carnelian next to them on your altar, then repeat the enchantment three times:

Vibes of positivity,
Surround me with your energy
Of joyous opportunity,
With harm to none and three by three.

5. Allow the candle to burn down fully and charge your carnelian, and say:

I wish it, and so it is!

6. Close your magick circle and remember to ground yourself.

7. Keep your carnelian somewhere prominent for a daily reminder of all the joyous opportunities life holds for you in abundance, and allow the energy of positive vibes to fill your home and your heart.

Action

Once you have performed this ritual, do something positive: go for a walk in the sunshine, or - my personal favorite - pop on your positive vibes playlist, sing along, and dance like no one is watching! Perform this ritual whenever you feel the need to keep the positive energies flowing.

⋆ Enchanted Gingerbread Cookies ⋆

Purpose

Budding kitchen witches will adore this magickal recipe. With sweet spices and ginger, these cookies remind us that variety is the 'spice of life'! Our zest for life is enhanced by balance, and a little bit of what you fancy is fine - and very good for you in moderation! So don't stress about the sugar or the carbs! Satisfy your sweet tooth and allow yourself to take a big bite out of life and enjoy what makes you happy! These little gingerbread positivity peeps are fun to make with kids, and they also make nice gifts for friends and family. If you've any dietary requirements, you can find any simple gingerbread recipe online to suit.

Lunar Phase

Any

Ingredients

~ Orange spell candle (to set on your kitchen windowsill while you work)

~ 12¼oz/350g of plain flour (plus extra for rolling out the dough)

~ 1 tsp bicarbonate of soda

~ 2 tsp ground ginger

~ 1 tsp ground cinnamon

~ A pinch of ground allspice

~ 4½oz/125g softened butter

~ 6¼oz/175g light soft brown sugar

~ 1 egg (free range)

~ 4 tbsp golden syrup

~ Waxed paper

~ Writing icing*

~ Sprinkles*

~ Few lengths of orange ribbon*

* Optional

Method

1. Light your orange spell candle and cast your magick circle.

2. Sift together the flour, bicarbonate of soda, and the spices, and pour them into a food processor. Add the butter and blend until the mixture resembles breadcrumbs. Add the sugar and pulse briefly until mixed.

3. In a separate bowl or jug, beat together the egg and the golden syrup, and add to the food processor, pulsing until the dough begins to clump together.

4. Tip the dough out, knead a few times, and say:

   Sugar, spice, and all things nice,
   I knead you once, I knead you thrice.
   I add my magick to this treat
   And as in life, each bite is sweet!

5. Wrap the dough in plastic wrap and pop it in the fridge to chill for about 15 minutes.

6. Meanwhile pre-heat the oven to 350°F/180°C (325°F /160°C for fan-assisted ovens) or Gas Mark 4, and line your baking trays with waxed paper.

7. On a floured surface, roll out the dough to about ¼in (0.5cm) thickness and use cutters to cut out the shapes; you can also make gingerbread people, or whatever other shapes take your fancy! Carefully place them on

the baking trays, making sure to leave a gap between each one.

8. Bake for 12–15 minutes or until golden. Remove the cookies from the oven and leave them to cool for 10 minutes on the trays before transferring them to wire racks.

9. Once completely cooled, you can decorate them with icing, sprinkles, or however you like, and if you made gingerbread people, you could tie some bright orange ribbons in bows around their necks.

10. Extinguish your candle, close your magick circle, and remember to ground yourself.

Action

Enjoy with friends and family, and a cup of zesty herbal Vitali-Tea. Bake these cookies whenever you're in the mood to spice things up and sweeten the soul.

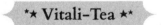

Purpose

Another ritual for the kitchen witch, Vitali-Tea is an extremely simple but very useful 'one ingredient' herbal tincture that was first served to me by a friend from Sri Lanka. It's a quick and easy charm that will help to remind you always to look for the positives in life. You may be surprised at how your half-empty cup is suddenly brimming with magick, joy, and optimism!

Lunar Phase
Any

Ingredients
~ Orange spell candle

~ Black teabag

~ Piece of fresh ginger

~ Milk and sugar to taste

Method
1. Cast your magick circle and inscribe the orange spell candle from wick to end with positive words or phrases, such as 'Vibrancy,' 'Joy,' or 'Optimism.' Then light it and set it on your kitchen windowsill.

2. Brew yourself a lovely cup of tea, and add a piece of fresh ginger.

3. Allow the tea to steep and place the cup next to your lit candle. Then, recite the charm:

Embrace all serendipity –
Change how I look, to what I see,
A life of opportunity

Filled with positivity
So harm to none and three by three.
My cup is full, and mote it be,
That hope and zest and energy
Enchant this sweet Vitali-Tea!

4. Enjoy your tea, allow the candle to burn down fully, and say:

I wish it, and so it is!

5. Close your magick circle and remember to ground yourself.

Action

Within the next hour do something invigorating: take a brisk walk, a bicycle ride, or a high-energy exercise class. Make your Vitali-Tea ritual part of your weekly routine and incorporate invigorating and energizing activities into your weekly habits to keep your mind and body optimized for health and positivity.

WISHES FOR LOVE, SEX, & BEAUTY

'Yes, I understand your spells – your sex magic – at least, I know this: all lights dim when you walk in...'

JOHN GEDDES

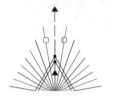

Magickal Correspondences

Key word: Sexuality
Color: Red
Earth Treasure: Garnet
Nature Gift: Sycamore seed
Herb or spice: Cinnamon
Flower or plant: Red rose
Incense: Patchouli
Essential oil: Ylang-ylang

⋆ Magickal Massage Oil ⋆

Purpose

Blend your own Magickal Massage Oil and spend a sensual, seductive evening with your lover. By enchanting your massage oil and allowing your partner to use it with you, you'll instantly reignite the passion you have for each other, and in that moment, you'll become completely irresistible to them, and they to you. Prepare for sparks to fly and for a few fireworks – this oil is strong stuff!

Be sure to temper the sexual energy of the red roses and cinnamon with the pink rose petals and candles to bring a balance of desire and tender romance. If you're single and looking for love, this is also a wonderful oil to use yourself after you shower and before you hit the town to attract a potential new mate. You can use the oil to anoint and dress spell candles for other love rituals, too.

Lunar Phase

New or Waxing Moon

Ingredients

~ Pink spell candle

~ Red spell candle

~ Patchouli incense*

~ Pestle and mortar or herb-chopper

~ 13 red and pink rose petals (fresh or dried)

~ Carrier massage oil (enough to fill the bottle you're making)

~ Jug

~ 3 pinches of ground cinnamon

~ 3 drops of rose essential oil

~ 3 drops of ylang-ylang essential oil

~ Plastic funnel

~ Empty small bottle with lid (well rinsed and dried)

~ Label and red pen

* Optional

Method

1. Cast your magick circle, set your altar, and light the pink and red spell candles side by side – leaving yourself an area of space to work, and the Patchouli incense (if using).

2. As the candles burn, set to work finely chopping or grinding your rose petals.

3. Add the carrier massage oil to the jug and mix in the petals, cinnamon, and essential oils.

4. Stir the mixture nine times deosil, chanting the verse each time as you do:

> *Red for passion, pink for love,*
> *Roses for romance.*
> *I blend this spell and wish it well,*
> *And leave nothing to chance!*

5. Using the funnel, pour the oil into your bottle and replace the cap tightly.

6. Write your magickal name and 'Love Oil' in red and label the bottle.

7. Leave the Magickal Massage Oil bottle on your altar to charge until the candles have completely burned out.

8. Close your magick circle and remember to ground yourself.

Action

If you plan to use the Magickal Massage Oil with a partner, arrange a date night and add some extra romance to your room with few special touches – pink and red candles, long-stemmed roses, or rose petals on the bed. Garnet crystals and patchouli and rose incense will all enhance the mood (and the magick!).

Just remember to let your partner know that your massage oil is a little bit magickal, and make sure they don't mind! Invite them to explore your body with a relaxing massage and offer to reciprocate, too. Relax and enjoy a beautiful, sensual experience together. If you're looking for love, arrange a night out with friends and dab a little Love Oil in place of your usual fragrance to attract plenty of new admirers.

★ A True Love Wish ★

Purpose

If you're looking for true love, this spell works like a charm. Apples have long been associated with love and sex magick, and they're also a symbol of fertility – it's the sweet fruit of life, bearing resemblance to the feminine womb with the seeds of new life within. The next time you eat an apple, be sure to save the seeds (the ones from a red apple are best).

It's important you take your time with this spell, and don't rush. Think about all the qualities and attributes you're looking for in your perfect mate. This spell is potent, so you want to be sure that you're getting right to the heart of what really matters to you in a relationship and keeping your vibes positive. For example, if being bored in bed is a deal-breaker, phrase it positively on your wish list and ask for 'Someone who is adventurous and passionate in bed.'

Think about age, hobbies, job, education, politics, children, location, and anything else that's important to you in a partner. You can literally describe to the Universe your ideal dream person when you perform this spell. Just bear in mind that while the Universe will send you your dream guy or girl, they'll still be human and they'll still have flaws. Nobody is completely perfect – including us!

Lunar Phase

New or Waxing Moon

Ingredients

~ Red spell candle (for a passionate heart)

~ Pink spell candle (for a romantic soul)

~ White spell candle (for honesty and pure intentions)

~ Your WishCraft journal and a red pen

~ 9 apple pips

~ Garnet tumblestone

~ Red spell bag

Method

1. Set your altar out, cast your magick circle, and inscribe the spell candles from wick to end for their symbolic meanings as above.

2. Take some time to write your 'perfect partner' wish list in your journal- be positive and get specific!

3. Arrange the apple pips in the shape of a love heart and place your garnet in the center.

4. Lay your left hand over your garnet and recite the invocation:

> *With these words bring what I seek,*
> *Of true love's kiss is what I speak.*
> *Drawn to me a lover new*
> *Of honor, truth, and beauty too.*
> *A love of tender sweet embrace,*
> *A gentle heart, and fair of face.*
> *This soulful spirit drawn to me*
> *Is one who knows we're meant to be.*
> *Our passions burn a lasting fire,*
> *We are each other's heart's desire.*
> *So as these apple pips I cast,*
> *Bring me a love, whose love will last.*
> *By the power of three times three*
> *With harm to none, and mote it be!*

5. Gather up your garnet and the apple pips and pop them into a red spell bag.

6. Enchant your charm by passing it around the candles three times deosil and say:

> *I wish it, and so it is!*

7. Allow the candles to burn down and then close your magickal circle and remember to ground yourself.

8. Keep the true love charm with you – especially on dates!

Action

Arrange a night out with the girls, set up a new dating profile online, or head to a new coffee shop on your next work break. Join a course or take up a new hobby – get out and about, meet new people, and make new friends. You might just be surprised at where your true love has been waiting for you to find them all along. You can repeat this spell as many times as you need to at each New Moon to remind the Universe of your intentions. The Universe may take a little time to fulfill your wish list, but trust that your true love is out there right now searching for you too!

✶ The Queen of Hearts ✶

Purpose

Looking for love? Want all eyes on you in the club? If you're in need of a confidence boost when it comes to attracting some new admirers, then this is the perfect ritual for you. The Queen of Hearts is the girl who everyone notices when she walks into a room. She's beautiful, captivating, seductive, and self-assured. She can have her pick of admirers and because she knows her worth, she chooses only the absolute cream of the crop.

Lunar Phase

New, Waxing, or Full Moon

Ingredients

~ Red spell candle

~ Garnet tumblestone

~ Queen of Hearts playing card (draw one if you don't have one, or print one out from a picture online)

~ Red marker or ballpoint pen

~ Ylang-ylang essential oil or your personal blend of Love Oil

Method

1. Set your altar and cast your magick circle.

2. Inscribe the red spell candle with the words 'Queen of Hearts' wick to end, and inscribe your magickal name on the opposite side.

3. Write your magickal name across the Queen of Hearts playing card.

4. Anoint the candle with ylang-ylang oil or your own magickal Love Oil blend.

5. Hold the candle in your left hand as you bless it with the powers and properties of love, beauty, and confidence.

6. Light it, and pass your garnet around the candle flame three times deosil as you recite the incantation:

> Queen of Hearts,
> Queen of Hearts,
> Bless me with your skillful arts
> Of beauty, love, and confidence.
> They see me sway and watch me dance,
> A beauty Queen whose heart is pure
> With confidence, so self-assured,
> A smile that bewitches all,
> A presence surely to enthrall.
> So many lovers to approve
> Which one should this beauty choose?
> For I am her and she is me,
> A Queen of Hearts for all to see!
> By the power of three by three,
> With harm to none, so mote it be!

7. Carefully take the candle and drip three drops of wax on the center or the 'heart' of the playing card.

8. Replace the candle in its holder, and once you're sure the wax has cooled, place your left hand on the Queen of Hearts, hold the garnet in your right hand, and meditate on the flame.

9. Daydream about walking into a room full of sexy strangers and having all eyes on you. You're the most gorgeous girl there! Imagine how you feel and how you walk; how you dance and how you smile; and how it feels to be confident, assured, and having so much fun! Notice how, of all the strangers, only the ones who seem the most attractive and interesting to you approach, and how good it feels to strike up an enjoyable conversation with them.

10. When you feel ready, blow out the candle and say:

I wish it, and so it is!

11. Remember to close your magick circle and ground yourself.

Action

Pop the Queen of Hearts card into your purse and keep it with you whenever you feel like being the center of attention. Arrange a girls' night out or attend a class, event, or place where you know there will be lots of people. For an extra boost of confidence, wear something red (even lipstick!), and don't be too surprised if you come home with a few numbers!

WISHES FOR SELF-CARE & FRIENDSHIPS

'When a witch embodies self-love, her energy becomes magnetic and her sense of possibility becomes contagious.'

DACHA AVELIN

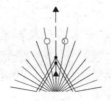

Magickal Correspondences

Key word: Affection

Color: Pink

Earth Treasure: Rose quartz

Nature Gift: Black and white feather

Herb or spice: Rosemary

Flower or plant: Pink rose

Incense: Apple blossom

Essential oil: Vanilla

⋆★ Self-Love Bath ★⋆

Purpose

I love this ritual! If I could do it every day I would. I found it a bit weird at first but loving and appreciating my body has made a massive difference to my health and wellbeing both physically *and* emotionally. The Universe is always listening, and when we love and appreciate ourselves deeply, we attract more love and appreciation into our lives. This is also a fab way of treating ourselves to a good pamper.

Be sure to lock the bathroom door and hang up your 'Do Not Disturb' sign. Feel free to tell your partner and/or the kids that you're doing witchy stuff, and if they interrupt you they may accidentally be turned into a frog (that should give you a bit of peace and quiet!).

If you prefer to use scented candles, the best fragrances for this spell are rose, strawberry, apple, and vanilla. I use a bath oil with real gold leaf in it and scented with turmeric root and coconut milk. I buy this online; it's very affordable, and I come out smelling divine and glittering like a Goddess. So go on, treat yourself, dive in, and show yourself some true love!

Lunar Phase

Any

Ingredients

~ Pink Himalayan salt or Epsom salt

~ Natural red or pink rose petals (fresh or dried)

~ Pink, red, and white candles

~ Rose quartz crystal/s

~ Cup of herbal tea or glass of wine

~ Your favorite bath oil or your own Love Oil blend

Method

1. You don't need to set up a full altar for this ritual, but do remember to cast your magick circle.

2. Run yourself a lovely warm bath, add the salts and petals, and light the candles.

3. You can place the rose quartz crystals around the bath or even add them to the water if you wish.

4. Step in, relax, and enjoy your tea or wine. Take in the soothing, loving vibrations of the rose quartz crystals and the warm glow of the candles.

5. When you're ready, pour a little oil into your hands and massage each part of your body you can reach, from head to toe. As you work, thank each part out loud (although you can whisper if you're worried about anyone overhearing!).

My lovely legs, thank you for supporting me when I walk.
My lovely hands, thank you for allowing
me to create, touch, and feel.
My lovely heart, thank you for beating
and keeping me alive.
My lovely stretch marks and scars, thank you for
reminding me of how I have grown, the life I have
sustained and the battles I have overcome.
My lovely boobs, thank you for looking
awesome in that new top I just bought.

6. And so on...

7. Then once you feel ready, say:

By the power of three by three,
I wish to love myself, for me!

8. Remember, this is your self-love ritual, so feel free to massage wherever you feel comfortable and don't feel the need to miss anywhere out. The more love and appreciation we can show our bodies, the healthier and happier we become.

9. Once you've finished your bath (and before you become a prune!), extinguish the candles and say:

I wish it, and so it is!

10. Close your magick circle and remember to ground yourself.

Action

Relax and enjoy! #Bliss

⋆★ Goddess Circle Wishing Ritual ★⋆

Purpose

This ritual is awesome to do with your girlfriends. Consider your girls as your Goddess circle; celebrate your femininity and bond over your achievements together. You're never too old to have a slumber party and now that you're grown-ups, you get to have sleepovers with wine!

Lunar Phase

New, Waxing, or Full Moon

Ingredients

~ Apple blossom incense

~ For each Goddess:

  - Pink spell candle

  - Pink ribbon

- Pink spell bag

- Pink rose quartz crystal

~ Small dish of rosemary (finely chopped, fresh or dried)

~ Glass of red or rosé sparkling wine (or apple or grape juice if you're not drinking alcohol)

~ Pajamas*

* Optional but comfy!

Method

1. Start by casting your magick circle in the usual way. Light your altar candle, along with the apple blossom incense, and all sit comfortably around the altar with the spell ingredients at the center.

2. Ask each Goddess to inscribe their name on their pink spell candle from wick to end, and the word 'Friendship.'

3. Once the candles are named and inscribed, pass them one place to the Goddess on the right (or exchange them if there's two of you).

4. Get each Goddess to tie a pink ribbon around the middle of the candle in a bow to signify their friendship, then pass the candle back.

5. Start with yourself and working deosil, each take a small pinch of rosemary and sprinkle it over the altar candle flame.

6. Take your pink crystals in your left hands, and with your friendship candles in your right, bring them all together to light them at the same time from the altar candle.

7. All hold both hands high in the air and say:

> *Our friendship circle we now cast,*
> *With friendship ties we mean to last.*
> *By the light of stars and Moon and Sun,*
> *We're strong together and as one.*
> *With love and light and three by three*
> *And harm to none so mote it be!*

8. Around the circle, one by one (you go first, followed by the Goddess on your right), blow out your candle, raise the glass of wine or juice, and say:

> *I honor my Goddesses and wish them*
> *health, abundance, and happiness!*

9. Take a sip and pass the glass on to the next Goddess. The last Goddess should finish the drink!

10. Pop your friendship crystals in pretty pink satin or organza spell bags, and each keep one as a sweet reminder of your amazing friendships.

11. Close your magick circle and remember to ground yourselves.

Action

Watch a movie, eat popcorn and nachos and ice cream, tell each other how amazing you all are – and finish your bottle of wine!

★ Wishes of Self-Appreciation ★

Purpose

Perform this ritual often to deepen your appreciation of all the wonderful and good things you do in your life. The kinder you are to yourself, the more strength and energy you have to support others. Honor your own talents and achievements – from the super and sensational, to the little and lovely things you do every single day! Did you get through the day without having a meltdown at work? Did you get around to putting on a bra today? Did you smash your personal best at the gym? Appreciate yourself for it! You're truly amazing.

Lunar Phase

Any

Ingredients

~ Pink spell candle

~ Apple blossom incense

~ Your WishCraft journal and a pen

~ Pink rose

Method

1. For this ritual you can set your altar if you wish, or you can simply cast your magick circle.

2. Inscribe the pink spell candle with your magickal name and any words that sing to you: 'Self-love,' 'Kindness,' and 'Appreciation' are all fab!

3. Light the candle along with the apple blossom incense, and spend some quiet time writing in your journal and reflecting on everything you've achieved.

4. Open your heart to love for yourself and for others, and dedicate your rose to gratitude:

> *With thanks this rose I dedicate*
> *And deeply do appreciate*
> *All the goodness I have shared*
> *And all the people who have cared.*
> *So Love I send to them, and me,*
> *And as I wish it, it shall be!*

5. Blow out the candle, close your magick circle, and remember to ground yourself.

Action

Place your rose in a vase of water on a window ledge as a reminder of beauty within your own heart. Remember to practice self-care often, and talk to yourself as kindly as you would to others.

WISHES FOR ANIMALS & THE EARTH

'Everything is made out of Magic, leaves and trees, flowers
and birds, badgers and foxes and squirrels and people.'

FRANCES HODGSON BURNETT

Magickal Correspondences

Key word:	Nature
Color:	Brown
Earth Treasure:	Smoky quartz
Nature Gift:	Horse chestnut
Herb or spice:	Catnip
Flower or plant:	Calendula
Incense:	Musk
Essential oil:	Pine

⋆★ Pet Protection Wish ★⋆

Purpose

This simple pet protection spell can be used for any animal but it's especially useful for cats who like to go out on their own. As I've been writing this book, my two cats, Rhubarb and Crumble, have contributed often - usually by sitting on my keyboard and 'typing' things with their little paws. Sadly, I've had to edit them out as most of us don't speak cat, but I still reckon a little bit of their kitty magick has found its way into these pages.

It's probably best not to have your pet with you in the room when you cast this spell, due to the candles and the catnip! (Most larger pet stores sell catnip and you can also find it easily online.)

Lunar Phase

New Moon

Ingredients

~ Brown spell candle

~ Large matchbox or small plastic box with a lid

~ Cotton wool

~ Photograph of your pet or a few strands of their fur (naturally shed)

~ 3 pinches of dried catnip

~ Brown ribbon, natural string, or twine

Method

1. Under the light of the New Moon, set your altar and cast your magick circle.

2. Inscribe the brown spell candle with the word 'Protection' from wick to end, and the name of your pet or the animal you wish to protect.

3. Light the candle and fill the box or tub with cotton wool.

4. Place your left hand over the photograph or fur, and say:

> *Should they wish it, so it shall be,*
> *Safe by the power of three by three,*
> *[Your pet's name] the [cat/dog/rabbit, etc.],*
> *Protected be!*

5. Allow the candle to burn down until a small stub remains. Place the stub, along with the photo or fur, on top of the cotton wool. Sprinkle it with three pinches of catnip and replace the lid.

6. Tie up the box like a parcel, with the ribbon or strings crossing vertically and horizontally over and under, and secure on top with a bow.

7. Close your magick circle and remember to ground yourself.

8. Place the box somewhere secure and trust the safety of your four-legged or feathered friends to the Universe.

Action

Now would be a great time to check that all your pet's vaccinations and preventative treatments are up to date and arrange their annual health check with the vet.

⋆ A Wish for Wildlife ⋆

Purpose

Use this ritual to send protection and healing to wildlife and nature during times of need, or just whenever you feel like helping to heal the Earth.

Lunar Phase

New, Waxing, or Full Moon

Ingredients

~ Brown spell candle

~ Pine essential oil

~ Musk incense

~ Smoky quartz tumblestone

~ Horse chestnut (you can substitute this with any other nut or seed if you need to)

Method

1. Set your altar and cast your magick circle.

2. Anoint the brown spell candle with the pine essential oil from wick to end, then light the musk incense and the candle, and place the smoky quartz next to them.

3. Pass the horse chestnut three times deosil around the flame, and say:

> *Earth, Water, Fire, Air,*
> *Nature spirits, hear my prayer.*
> *Trees, flowers, birds, and bees,*
> *Rivers, forests, hills, and seas,*
> *Creatures big and critters small,*
> *Bless, heal, and protect them all!*
> *With harm to none and three by three,*
> *Should they wish it, so it shall be!*

4. Allow the candle to burn down completely, then close your magick circle and remember to ground yourself.

5. Bury the chestnut in the earth as a sign of your healing intentions, and place your smoky quartz on your windowsill where you can see it every day and be reminded of the beauty of the nature and wildlife all around you.

Action

Do something positive for nature or the planet. Plant some flowers for the bees, do some recycling, or organize a local clean-up. Make a commitment to waste less and think about practical ways to honor your promise. Or simply put some food out for the birds. It doesn't matter whether it's a small action or a bigger one, the Universe takes energy from your positive actions and wishes for nature and wildlife. Your vibrations of love and protection make a huge difference to the world around you.

★ A Seashell Spell ★

Purpose

This little enchantment is for sending help and protection specifically to the seas and oceans. We all know the importance of our oceans – without water, we simply would not exist. Not to mention the vital and vibrant marine habitats that are slowly being eroded by humankind.

With this ritual, you can spare a thought for our seas and the whole of our ecosystem. Sending loving and healing vibes to the waters of the world deepens our appreciation of our beautiful planet and forges our connection with the Cosmos, as we set our intentions to be kind and considerate human beings. A Full Moon Esbat is a great time to perform this spell, as the Moon is the ruler of our oceans.

Lunar Phase

Waxing or Full Moon

Ingredients

~ Light-blue spell candle

~ Brown spell candle

~ Seashell (if you don't have one, draw a simple symbol on a small piece of paper)

~ Small bowl of water

Method

1. Set your altar and cast your magick circle.

2. Inscribe the light-blue spell candle with the word 'Ocean' and some wishes you want to send to it (for example,

'Clean,' 'Healthy,' or 'Protected'). You can also spend time inscribing symbols on the candle to represent marine life such as shells and starfish.

3. Inscribe the brown spell candle with the words 'Mother Earth' from wick to end.

4. Place the two candles in separate holders about 6in (15cm) apart on your altar, and begin the spell by saying:

> *By the power of three by three,*
> *I cast this wish to protect the sea*
> *And all the life that dwells in She,*
> *With harm to none so mote it be!*

5. Repeat the spell three times, and each time move your brown and blue candles slightly closer together until they're next to each other, then say:

> *Mother Earth, I ask of you,*
> *Protect our oceans bright and blue.*

6. Pass the seashell around the flames three times deosil, blow the candles out, and say:

> *I wish it, and so it is!*

7. Close your magick circle and ground yourself.

8. You can place the seashell in the bowl of water and leave it outside overnight, or if you're lucky enough to live by the sea, take it and give it back to the ocean.

Action

The most important part of this ritual is taking an action, however small, to do your bit to help the sea. Chose responsibly sourced fish and do all that you can to reduce plastic waste. Don't wait until it's too late – make a commitment to help today and in return the Elementals of Water will help you work your wishes!

WISHES FOR MOVING ON & LETTING GO

'Our purpose here is to observe, to learn, to grow, to love… and then we return home.'

AUSTRALIAN ABORIGINAL PROVERB

Magickal Correspondences

Key words:	Releasing negativity
Color:	Black
Earth Treasure:	Black obsidian
Nature Gift:	Black feathers
Herb or spice:	Black pepper
Flower or plant:	Mourning bride (scabiosa)
Incense:	Sandalwood
Essential oil:	Rue

⋆ A Wish for Loved Ones Lost ⋆

Purpose

It's a sad fact of life that sometimes we lose those we love the most. This spell was created to help ease the emotions of a loved one (human or animal) transitioning and passing on, but it can equally be used to soothe the pain of a relationship ending. It works well if performed after you've worked through some forgiveness rituals.

If you're performing this ritual following a relationship breakdown, as you speak the spell, remember the good aspects of the relationship or person, and what the relationship has taught you. Be thankful for those aspects as this will help heal your heart much faster. When a loved one dies or leaves (or puts you in a position where you cannot but ask them to leave) it's also natural to feel anger. From forgiveness comes love – albeit love from a different place in a heart that's healed – allowing you to move forward with renewed hope, positivity, and understanding.

Let the words of this spell wash over your heart, healing the wounds and filling it with fond memories, and accept that endings are only ever new beginnings. The Full Moon lends the most power to this ritual.

Lunar Phase

Full or Waning Moon

Ingredients

~ Black spell candle

~ Rue essential oil*

~ Sandalwood incense*

~ 1 mourning bride flower (if you can't find a mourning bride, a single crimson rose will also work)

* Optional but very helpful

Method

1. Inscribe the black spell candle from end to wick with the emotions you wish to let go of – these might be 'Grief,' 'Anger,' 'Sadness,' or 'Loneliness' – and if using the rue essential oil, anoint your candle in the same direction.

2. Before you light it, hold the candle between your hands, close your eyes, and spend a few moments focusing on pouring all the emotions from your heart into it.

3. When you're ready, place your candle in a holder, light it and the sandalwood incense, and say:

> *I loved you then, I love you still,*
> *I know my heart will heal.*

When sadness comes deep in the night,
There is no fear to feel.
As time goes by, the wheel turns,
And even though you're gone,
We loved and laughed and lived to learn,
We'll sleep and be reborn.
Betwixt, Between, the liminal,
A place we both can dwell,
So when I fall asleep and dream
I find us whole and well.
We dance together through the stars
And soar back down to Earth,
And when I wake, I'm not alone
My heart is filled with hope.

4. Blow out the candle and open a window, allowing the thin swirl of smoke to be set free like a soul on the breeze. As the smoke swirls and disappears through the open window, imagine it's your grief and sadness being gently blown away, and say:

I wish it, and so it is!

5. Close your magick circle and spend some extra time grounding yourself.

Action

Take the mourning bride flower or rose outside – to a garden or park – and find somewhere pretty to lay your flower, and your grief, to rest. As you do this, it's important to take a moment to breathe – then turn away and don't look back. You're letting go of your grief and pain, not the soul you've lost. You'll always remember them (or the good aspects of them) with fondness and comfort. They want you to allow yourself to heal and move on.

Make yourself a soothing warm drink, play some uplifting music, call a friend, or plan a getaway. Know that you're not alone, and that you can find your way through grief and sadness to joy, renewed hope, and love. If you feel it may help, reach out to a grief or relationship counselor, and seek professional support to aid your recovery.

Remember that the Universe helps us most when we take steps to help ourselves.

⋆★ A Wish to Release Negativity ★⋆

Purpose

This spell can help with letting go of any negative emotions that are holding you back. It's simple but powerful, and can help to release old hurts and bad vibes that interfere with your mood and magick! Remember, you can only work on your own negative emotions, not on other people's. Because like attracts like, the more positive a person you become, the more positivity you attract to surround yourself with. Sometimes, we may need to let go of certain people in our lives, as well as the negative emotions they inspire in us. Work on *yourself* to bring security, safety, and positivity into your life.

Lunar Phase
Waning Moon

Ingredients
~ Black spell candle

~ Sandalwood incense

~ White wax crayon or pencil crayon

~ Black craft paper

~ Craft scissors

~ 3 pinches of black pepper

Method
1. Set your altar, cast your magick circle, and inscribe the black spell candle with the negative emotion you want to release from end to wick (for example, 'fear,' 'anger,' or 'jealousy'). It's best to work on only one emotion at a time.

2. Light the black spell candle and sandalwood incense.

3. With the white pencil or crayon, write the emotion on the black paper in large letters.

4. Take the craft scissors and begin to cut and re-cut the paper until you have a small pile of confetti.

5. Take three pinches of black pepper and sprinkle them over the candle flame from a height, repeating the verse three times:

> *This [emotion] does not serve me,*
> *I release and let it go,*
> *To make room for the positive,*
> *To flourish and to flow.*

6. As the candle burns down, meditate on the flame and ask the Universe to help you find a way to deal with and release the negative emotion that no longer serves you.

7. Once the candle has burned down fully, say:

> *I wish it, and so it is!*

8. If you have a chiminea or similar, burn the confetti outside. If this isn't an option, be sure to recycle your confetti and remove it from your home as soon as you can.

9. Close your magick circle and remember to ground yourself.

Action

Do something positive that makes you feel happy or inspired! Read an inspirational book, watch an uplifting movie, or print out and pin up a positive quote somewhere you'll see it every day. Take a walk in the sunshine, spend some time with family and friends, or choose a positivity or self-love ritual to perform.

★ A Heartsease Wish ★

Purpose

This ritual helps to heal a rift after an argument and mend a broken heart. Whether it's a partner, friend, or family member that you've fallen out with, this spell will gently allow you to release any negative energy and move forward with positivity and love, whether that be together or apart.

Remember, you should never try and directly influence another person's will or wishes. With this spell, you're simply letting the Universe know that you're ready to forgive and heal, and open your heart to love, kindness, and compassion, with the intention that anyone else affected will also be able to heal and move on. Sometimes forgiveness can be hard, but trust that the Universe will make sure you receive what you give out, in ways you may not even yet imagine.

Lunar Phase

Full or Waning Moon

Ingredients

~ Black spell candle

~ Sandalwood incense

~ Black craft paper

~ Sewing needle

~ Pink thread

~ Black obsidian tumblestone

Method

1. Set your altar and cast your magick circle.

2. Light the black spell candle and sandalwood incense.

3. Cut two love-heart shapes from the black craft paper.

4. Take each heart one at a time, fold it vertically in half, and carefully stitch it together – it doesn't matter how or which stitches you use, you are simply symbolically mending the hearts. Be careful not to stitch the two hearts together, as this could inspire a very different outcome and not one which might be the best for all concerned – including you!

5. As you work, say the following verse:

I sew these hearts to mend them
And heal the rifts we made.
Forgiveness will repair them
And allow the wounds to fade.

6. Next, take the sewn hearts in your left hand, and the black obsidian tumblestone in your right. Focus on the candle flame and feel any negativity draining into the black obsidian, and the love from the hearts you've mended flowing freely back into your own.

7. Without expectation or condition, forgive the person who has upset or angered you – and forgive yourself.

8. Once you feel ready, blow out your candle and say:

I wish it, and so it is!

9. Open a window to allow the smoke to disperse and release the negativity from your space.

10. If you can, bury the black obsidian somewhere outside. If you can't do this, cleanse it in a bowl of water and pour the water away.

11. Close your magick circle and remember to ground yourself.

Action

Do a kind and loving thing. This could be anything from sending a card to a friend, to making a small donation to charity, or even practicing some self-care. Put unconditional kindness and love out into the world, and that's exactly what you'll receive back - threefold!

WISHES FOR SUNSHINE & SUMMERTIME

'Let us dance in the sun, wearing
wild flowers in our hair…'

SUSAN POLIS SCHUTZ

Magickal Correspondences

Key words:	Masculinity; energy
Color:	Gold
Earth Treasure:	Sunstone
Nature Gift:	Autumn or fall leaves
Herb or spice:	Saffron
Flower or plant:	Sunflower
Incense:	Myrrh
Essential oil:	Citrus fruits

⋆★ A Pocketful of Sunshine ★⋆

Purpose

Sunshine is nature's antidepressant, and if, like me, you live somewhere in the world where sunshine can often be scarce, this ritual can bring an instant fix of the gold stuff into your life. If you suffer with SAD (Seasonal Affective Disorder), this charm can be especially helpful. Even those of us who see the Sun every day can benefit from the happy boost of energy this spell brings.

It used to be believed that sunstone was little pieces of the Sun that had fallen to Earth, and myrrh was burned by the ancient Egyptians as an offering to Ra, the Sun God. This ritual packs as many sunny vibes as possible into one charm – so that you can quite literally carry the sunshine around in your pocket and harness the power of solar energy on even the darkest and rainiest of days!

Lunar Phase

Any

Ingredients

~ Myrrh incense

~ Gold spell candle

~ 3 drops of citrus essential oil

~ Gold or yellow spell bag

~ Sunstone tumblestone

~ A few strands of saffron

~ 3 sunflower seeds

~ 3 sunflower petals (or any other bright yellow flowers with small petals - even a dandelion will do the trick!)

Method

1. Set your altar and cast your magick circle.

2. Light the myrrh incense and anoint the gold spell candle with the citrus oil from wick to end. Light the candle.

3. Place the rest of the ingredients into the spell bag, and pass it around the candle flame three times deosil.

4. Enchant your charm with sunshine by saying:

> *Sunshine warm and sunshine bright,*
> *Fill me with your golden light.*
> *Lend to me your happy rays*
> *To chase away my rainy days.*
> *And by the power of three by three,*
> *Imbue this charm with majesty.*
> *With harm to none, so 'twill be done,*
> *This little charm is filled with Sun!*

5. Allow the candle to burn down fully, then close your magick circle and remember to ground yourself.

Action

Carry your charm in your pocket or purse for a little burst of sunshine and positive energy whenever you feel eclipsed by shadows.

★ Summery Solar Tea ★

Purpose

This delicious iced tea – infused with delicate flavors, sunshine, and, of course, a little bit of magick – makes a wonderful drink to sip on a sunny day and share with friends. A Kilner or mason jar is useful for this recipe, but any other large glass jar with a lid will work fine – just make sure it's well washed with no lingering scents that could ruin your tea. You can also use loose-leaf tea for this, which does taste better – just remember that you'll need a strainer for your enchanted tea!

Lunar Phase

Any

Ingredients

~ Gold spell candle

~ 3-4 black tea bags

~ Large jar with lid

~ Large jug filled with enough cold or tepid water to fill the jar

~ Sugar to taste

~ Ice cubes

~ 1 orange, sliced

~ 1 lemon, sliced

~ Wooden spoon

Method

1. You don't need your altar for this spell; simply cast your magick circle and light the gold spell candle on a windowsill while you prepare your tea.

2. Pop the tea bags in the jar and fill to the top with cold or tepid water (not boiling water!)

3. Replace the lid tightly, give the jar a gentle shake, and place it in a sunny spot outside, preferably on a hard surface (such as a glass table or a patio). Say:

Of this solar tea we drink,
To celebrate the Sun.
Enchanted be with golden light and warmth,
His work be done!

4. Allow the candle to burn down completely (or until one hour has passed).

5. Bring the tea back inside and give it another gentle shake. Don't worry if it's gone very dark as you can always add a little more water.

6. Pour the tea from the jar into the large jug (through a strainer if using loose-leaf tea) and add sugar to taste.

7. Add some ice, slices of fresh lemon and orange, and give everything a good stir with the wooden spoon.

8. Close your magick circle and remember to ground yourself.

9. Pour into glasses and serve straight away – drink a toast to the Sun!

Action

To acknowledge the Sun's work in the cycle of growth and life, be sure to add your used teabags or tea leaves to your compost heap, or your flower borders or pots (just tear the teabags open) or even sprinkle on your lawn to give the grass a boost.

⋆★ A Summer Solstice Wish ★⋆

Purpose

If you can, perform this ritual outside on the Summer Solstice to honor the Sun and the ever-turning wheel of life.

Lunar Phase

Any

Ingredients

~ Gold spell candle

~ Citrus essential oil

~ Myrrh incense

~ Sharp knife

~ 1 fresh orange

~ 3 sunflower seeds

~ 3 pinches of saffron

~ 1 sunflower (or any yellow flower)

Method

1. Set your altar and cast your magick circle. Anoint your gold spell candle from end to wick with the citrus

essential oil, and light it along with the myrrh incense to honor the Sun.

2. Carefully make a small slit in your orange, large enough so that you can push the sunflower seeds and the saffron inside it.

3. Place your orange (the 'Sun') and the sunflower next to your candle and say:

God of Sunshine, God of Light,
I honor you this summer's night,
With thanks for all the warmth you bring
To light our lives with sunny things.
As rain does wash the summer's dust
And green leaves fall to autumn rust,
Our year's hard work you've helped to grow
And soon now time to reap the sow.
So as your rays begin to soften,
With longer nights that come more often,
In spring I'll wait for you to rise
And watch for you with golden eyes.
Your work here for the year now done,
I turn to stars, as sleeps the Sun.

4. Allow your candle to burn down fully, and place your orange and the sunflower offering under your favorite tree.

5. Close your magick circle and remember to ground yourself.

Action

As the nights draw in and the days begin to shorten, take time to reflect on all you've achieved so far this year and practice gratitude. Look forward to harvesting the fruits of your labors and reaping the rewards of the plans you've made that will soon come to fruition. Soon it will be time to take stock, celebrate the harvests, begin to wind down for the winter, and make preparations and plans again for the new year ahead!

Afterword:
Follow Your Heart

'Then close your eyes and tap your
heels together three times.'

GLINDA, *The Wizard of Oz*

I hope that you've enjoyed trying WishCraft for yourself, and that you're feeling as excited as I am about what the future holds. Of course, the wishing spells in this little book are just a few examples of how you can tweak the shimmering spider's web to manifest your most magickal desires. Now that you're a Mistress of the basics, you can begin to experiment with WishCraft by creating your own rituals and casting the wishes that have the most meaning for you. Follow the link on the resources page (*see page 279*) to the Magickal Correspondences Quick Reference Guide I've created to help you begin crafting your own spells!

You've earned those glittery red slippers, so wear them with pride! You're a powerful woman with magick in her heart and a sparkle in her step; a woman who knows how to create the life she dreams of - on her own terms. And now that you've unlocked the door to your inner witchy wisdom, a lifetime of endless and abundant opportunity awaits. The end of this book is in fact just the beginning of your personal magickal journey, and *my* final wish is one for you: that your life is forever filled with passion, purpose, magick, and miracles.

And as you wish it, so it shall be!

Brightest Blessings,

Sakura xXx

Resources:
Something 'Wicked'
This Way Comes

'Everyone deserves a chance to fly!'

ELPHABA, *WICKED*

The WishCraft Academy for Wickedly Successful Women

Over at the WishCraft Academy, you'll find a community of like-minded women to connect with who are using WishCraft to create positive change in their lives. You'll also find a bunch of awesome free book bonuses to download and print – they will help you along on your journey to becoming a Wickedly Successful Witch!

Go online now for:

★ Your personal Secret Soul Signature profile

★ Your Magickal Correspondences Quick Reference Guide

★ Inspirational playlists, affirmations, and WishCraft tips

www.wishcraft.academy

f @WishCraftAcademy

⬜ wishcraft.academy

#WickedWitches

Acknowledgments

On this day I thank my lucky stars...

For my publisher. Hay House, and all the team who've worked so hard on *WishCraft*. Especially to Michelle Pilley for this wonderful and unexpected opportunity, and to commissioning editors Elaine O'Neill and Emily Arbis, for all your encouragement and help in getting my first submission where it needed to be. A massive thank you to my copy editor, Susie Bertinshaw, for somehow magickally making my scribbling fit the word count – and for brightening my day with chats about cats, stargazing, and 'underpants.' To Kari Brownlie for the gorgeous cover, and to Leanne Siu Anastasi for making the book look so beautiful. To Jo Burgess for managing the promotion and publicity, and to managing editor Julie Oughton for making the magick happen. I owe you all a huge box of Enchanted Gingerbread Cookies!

For all the amazing people I've been blessed to have in my life, who whispered to oceans and showed me the stars.

With special thanks for all your love and support to Mom – the Wickedest Witch in the West Midlands – and Dad, the original Del-Boy. To Auntie Di, Cee, Vicky, and Nadine for your kind words of encouragement. To my big brother Phil, for showing me that your past need not define your future. To Nic, Kelly, and Erin – the Three Amigos – for the gifts, the GIFs and the giggles. To Rob, for being the best friend a girl could ever wish for! And to Ben, for believing in my magick (but not necessarily the Gnomes). I love you all.

For all the authors of the quotes and wise words that pepper these pages, and for the Hay House writers who have been an inspiration and a guiding light, especially Denise DT the Lucky Bee, and the lovely Louise – a guardian angel in every sense of the word.

For all the wonderful witches and Wickedly Successful Women who have shared their work and their wisdom – thank you for teaching me so much.

For you, dear reader, for helping to make the world a place where any woman can make her wildest dreams and wishes come true!

ABOUT THE AUTHOR

Sakura Fox is an entrepreneur, an author and a witch. Her approach to WishCraft and witchcraft is accessible, modern, and fun. She is the founder of the WishCraft Academy, an online resource for women who want to explore the world of magickal manifesting without having to perform complex ceremonies or complicated spells. Sakura is passionate about inspiring women to have the confidence to become the Mistresses of their own destiny through her teaching, which combines spiritual development, self-appreciation and powerful Cosmic communication.

When she isn't focussed on WishCraft, Sakura enjoys horse-riding, home-making, and a pink Gin fizz with friends. She lives in rural South Wales, by the sea, with her two grown-up daughters and their cats, Rhubarb and Crumble.

f @WishCraftAcademy

⊙ wishcraft.academy

🐦 @WishCraft_AC

🅿 WishCraftAcademy

www.wishcraft.academy